MW01614965

O Allah,

send prayers upon our master Muhammad, the opener of what was closed, and the seal of what had preceded, the helper of the truth by the Truth, and the guide to Your straight path. May Allah send prayers upon his Family according to his grandeur and magnificent rank.

-Salāt al-Fātīh

Title: Miracles of the Prophet Muhammad ﷺ

ISBN: 978-1-952306-17-4

first edition | January 2022

Author: Qāḍi 'Iyād b. Mūsa al-Yahsubi
Translator: jody mcintyre
Proofreading: wordsmiths
Typesetting: igp consulting | www.igpconsulting.com
Distribution: www.sattaurpublishing.com

www.imamghazalipublishing.com

MIRACLES *of the* PROPHET MUHAMMAD ﷺ

Qāḍi ʿIyād b. Mūsa al-Yahsubi

Contents

Publisher's Message

All praise is due to Allah, the First; without a beginning, and the Last; without an end. Peace and prayers be upon the Prophet Muhammad ﷺ, the first Prophet on the Day of Judgement to offer intercession despite being the last Prophet sent, and upon his pure family, his blessed Companions, and all who follow their way upon the path of righteousness, until the day intercession begins with none other than the Prophet Muhammad ﷺ.

Al-Shifā bi Taʿrīf Ḥuqūq al-Muṣṭafā, directly translated as, 'The Remedy (or Cure) Through Recognizing the Rights of the Chosen One', is one of the most celebrated works in the genre of Shamā'il. It stands uniquely amongst the works of Qāḍī ʿIyād as his most celebrated effort–with many surviving manuscripts and commentaries found throughout the Islamic world. Shamā'il is a genre of works that deals with the life, characteristics, and descriptions of the Prophet ﷺ and his station. There are many works in this genre, the most celebrated of which is *Al-Shamā'il al-Muḥammadiyyah*, which Imam Ghazali Publishing recently translated and published. Other works include commentaries and summaries of that nature, or hagiographical poems that recount the biography of the Prophet ﷺ and render praise to the Prophetic station.

However, *Al-Shifā*, as it is called for short, stands alone as perhaps the most thorough work in this genre, dealing with both the descriptions of the Prophet ﷺ, his station and his perfections, and with the rulings pertaining to one's belief and treatment of him ﷺ. It is exhaustive in its treatment of the subject, expounding on topics that range from Allah's praise of the Prophet ﷺ and his status and station before Him, to the obligation of loving him and what that entails. In short, the uniqueness of this work can be attributed to its holistic coverage of the Messenger ﷺ. Historically, this work took on a form of sacredness and was revered throughout the Muslim world. With that in mind, the Qāḍī's intention for this blessed work was more so to address, what he understood as, a real and practical need in his society. In today's context, it is our intention to continue the spirit of his desire outlined for us in his introduction:

> You have repeatedly asked me to write something which gathers together all that is necessary to acquaint the reader with the true stature of the Prophet, peace and blessings be upon him, with the esteem and respect which is due to him, and with the verdict regarding anyone who does not fulfill what his stature demands or who attempts to denigrate his supreme status—even by as much as a nail-paring. I have been asked to compile what our forebears and imams have said on this subject, and I will amplify it with *ayāt* from the Qur'an and other examples...Writing about this calls for the evaluation of the primary sources, examination of secondary sources, and investigation of the depths and details of the science of what is necessary for the Prophet, what should be attributed to him, and what is forbidden or permissible in respect of him; and deep knowledge of Messenger-ship and Prophethood and of the love, intimate friendship and the special qualities of the sublime rank.[1]

Although it has previously been translated into English in its entirety,

1 Iyad ibn Musa, *Muhammad: Messenger of Allah: Ash-Shifā by Qadi 'Iyad* , translated by Aisha Abdarrahman Bewley, vi.

our intention with this series is to attempt to bring out, for our readers, some of the most relevant smaller, yet critically important, topics related to the Prophet ﷺ, his station, our duty towards him, and the benefit of loving him and fulfilling our duty towards him. Such a task has been made easier for us by the expert arrangement of the text in terms of its sections and subsections. Each larger section is divided into smaller subsections, which facilitates targeted publications that are small but great in benefit. It is our desire, with having isolated smaller and somewhat easier 'quick-reads', as they are called, that readers may be inspired to complete a full reading of the noble Qāḍī's entire work.

Talut Dawood
Imam Ghazali Publishing

Qāḍi ʻIyād b. Mūsa al-Yahsubi

The Imām, the unique Ḥāfiẓ, Shaykh al-Islām, ʻAllāmah, Qādḍi Abū al-Faḍl ʻIyād b. Mūsa b. ʻIyād b. ʻUmar b. Mūsa b. ʻIyād al-Yahsubi al-Andalūsi al-Sibti al-Māliki was born in the year 476/1083–84, six months after the Almoravid takeover of the city. His ancestors left Andalus for Fez and then settled in Ceuta. At the age of 22, Qāḍi ʻIyād obtained a license (*ijāzah*) from Ḥāfiẓ Abū ʻAlī al-Ghasāni. This allowed Qāḍi ʻIyād to take knowledge from him. The Qāḍi had otherwise not studied the Islāmic sciences at an early age.

He left Ceuta on two occasions, one of which was to travel to Andalus seeking out scholars with whom he could take knowledge. Between 507/1113 and 508/1114 the Qāḍi visited Cordoba, Almeria, Murcia, and Granada. During this time, he learned Ḥadith from the famed scholar, Qāḍi Abū ʻAlī b. Sukrah al-Sadafi. Qāḍi ʻIyād stayed with him closely. He also took Ḥadīth from Abū Baḥr b. al-ʻĀs, Muḥammad b. Ḥamdayn, Abū al-Ḥusayn Sirāj al-Saghīr, Abū Muḥammad b. ʻAttab, Hishām b. Aḥmad and many other scholars. He learned jurisprudence (*fiqh*) from Abū ʻAbdullah Muḥammad b. ʻIsa al-Tamīmī and Qāḍi Muḥammad b. ʻAbdullāh al-Masili.

The Qāḍi was first appointed judge of Ceuta in 515/1121 and served in his position until 531/1136. He would later serve again in Cueta from

539–543/1145–48. His tenure as a judge in Cueta was probably his most productive period; his casework created the foundations for his works in jurisprudence (*fiqh*). Khalaf b. Shakwal said of him:

> He is among the people of knowledge and polymaths, of great intelligence and understanding. He performed the duties of a judge in Ceuta for a long time, in which he earned a praiseworthy reputation. Then he travelled from there for a judgeship in Granada. However, he did not stay there long. Thereafter, he came to us in Cordoba and we took from him.

The jurist (*faqīh*) Muḥammad b. Ḥammadah al-Sibti said:

> The Qāḍi began training at the age of twenty-eight years and assumed judgeship at the age of thirty-five. He was lenient, but not weak, [and] fierce in defence of the truth. He learned jurisprudence (*fiqh*) from Abū 'Abdullah al-Tamīmī and accompanied Abū Isḥāq b. Ja'far. No one in Ceuta wrote more works than him during his time. He wrote the book 'Al-Shifā' fi Sharāf al-Mustafa', 'Tartīb al-Madārik wa Taqrīb al-Masālik fī Dhikr Fuqahā' Madhab Mālik', a multi-volume work, 'Kitāb al-'Aqīdah', 'Kitāb Sharḥ Ḥadīth Umm Zar'', the book 'Jāmi' al-Tārīkh' and others.

Many scholars narrate from Qāḍi 'Iyād. Among them are Imām 'Abdullah b. Muḥammad al-'Ashīri, Abū Ja'far b. al-Qasir al-Gharnāti, al-Ḥāfiẓ Khalaf b. Bashakwal, Abū Muḥammad b. 'Ubayd Allah al-Hijri, Muḥammad b. al-Ḥasan al-Jābirī and his son, Qāḍi Muḥammad b. 'Iyād, the Qāḍi of Denia (in Spain).

Qāḍi b. Khalkhan said, 'The teachers of Qāḍi 'Iyād number around one hundred. He passed away during Ramaḍan 544/December-January 1149–50.' Conversely, it has also been reported that he died in Jumada al-Ākhirah of the same year, in Marrakesh. His son passed away in the year 575 AH.

Ibn Bashakwal said, 'Qāḍi 'Iyād passed away to the west of his hometown, in the middle of the year 544 AH." His son, Qāḍi Muḥammad, said,

'He passed away in the middle of the night, on Friday 9 Jumada al-Ākhirah. He was buried in Marrakesh in the year 544 AH.'

I [al-Dhahabi] say, 'it has reached me that he was killed by an arrow for his denial that Ibn Tumart was infallible'.

Some of the Qāḍi's well-known works are:

1. Al-Shifā' bi Ta'rīf Ḥuqūq al-Mustafā – the Shifa' remains one of the most commentated books of Islām.
2. Tartīb al-Madārik wa Taqrīb al-Masālik li Ma'rifat A'lām Madhab Mālik.
3. Ikmāl al-Mu'lim bi Fawa'id Muslim – Qāḍi 'Iyād's own commentary was expounded upon heavily by Imām al-Nawawi in his commentary of Saḥiḥ Muslim.
4. Al-I'lām bi Ḥudūd Qawā'id al-Islām – a work on the five pillars of Islām.
5. Al-Ilma' ilā Ma'rifa Usūl al-Riwāyah wa Taqyīd al-Sama' – a detailed work on the science of Ḥadīth.
6. Mashāriq al-Anwār 'ala Saḥiḥ al-Athar – a work based on the Muwaṭā of Imām Mālik, Saḥiḥ Al-Bukhāri of Imām Bukhāri, and Saḥiḥ Muslim by Imām Muslim.
7. Al-Tanbihāt al-Mustanbaṭah 'ala al-Kutub al-Mudawwanah wa al-Mukhtalaṭah.
8. Daqā'iq al-Akhbar fi Dhikr al-Jannah wa al-Nār – a work describing the joys of Heaven (*Jannah*) and the horrors of Hell (*Jahannam*).

MIRACLES *of the* PROPHET MUHAMMAD ﷺ

Qāḍi ʿIyād b. Mūsa al-Yahsubi

The Miracles Allah Exalted Showed Through the Actions of the Prophet ﷺ, and the Noble and Dignified Characteristics He Honoured Him With

The reader should know that we did not compile this book for the one who denies the status of the Prophet ﷺ, nor the one who wants to find doubts in the miracles he performed. Therefore, we do not need to use this chapter to establish the evidence for these miracles and prove their authenticity in order to pre-empt and cut off the arguments of those who attempt to find doubts. Neither will we be delving into the conditions, challenges, and limitations in determining whether something is to be considered miraculous or not. Similarly, it is not necessary for us to detail the false arguments of those who deny that the laws and revelation that the Prophet ﷺ brought to mankind were to supersede any revelation before them, or the responses to those claims. Rather, we authored this section on the miracles of the Prophet ﷺ for the people of his religion – the ones who responded to his call and believed in his Prophethood – in order to reinforce their love for him, to encourage them to perform righteous actions, and to increase them in faith *(īmān)*.

Our intention in this chapter is to document the greatest miracles and signs, both of which indicate the greatness of the abilities that Allah has bestowed upon the Prophet ﷺ. We have presented those miracles that have been meticulously studied and possess the most authentic chains of transmission. And most of what has been transmitted is undisputedly authentic, or almost so, to which we have added some of the narrations found in the well-known books of reputable scholars.

If an equitable person reflects on what we have presented, from the beauty of his effect on people, the praiseworthiness of his life, the ingenuity of his knowledge, his ability to act with wisdom and understanding, the completeness of his speech and all his traits, whilst being a witness to the circumstances he lived in and the benefit in what he said, they would neither doubt the veracity of his Prophethood nor the truth of his call. And these characteristics alone are sufficient for a person to embrace Islam and to believe in the Prophet ﷺ.

We transmitted from Tirmidhī, Ibn Qāni', and others – with their chains of transmission – that 'Abdullāh ibn Salām said: "When the Messenger of Allah ﷺ arrived in Madinah, I came so that I would be able to see him. When I caught sight of his face, I knew that it was not the face of a liar."

This hadith was narrated to us from Abū 'Alī from Abū al-Ḥusayn al-Ṣayrafī and Abū al-Faḍl ibn Khayrūn, from Abū Ya'lā al-Baghdādī, from Abū 'Alā al-Sinjī, from Ibn Maḥbūb, from Tirmidhī, who said: "It was narrated to us from Muhammad ibn Bashshār, from 'Abd al-Wahhāb al-Thaqafī, Muhammad ibn Ja'far, Ibn Abī 'Adiyy, and Yaḥyā ibn Sa'īd, from 'Awf ibn Abī Jamīlah al-A'rābī, from Zurārah ibn Awfā, from 'Abdullāh ibn Salām."[2]

Abū Rimthah al-Taymī related: "I came to the Prophet ﷺ, and my son was with me. I was shown [the Prophet ﷺ], and when I saw him, I said: 'This is the Prophet of Allah ﷺ.'"

It was transmitted from Muslim, and others, from Ḍimād, that when he came to the Prophet ﷺ, he said: "Without doubt, all Praise and Gratitude is for Allah, we praise Him and seek refuge with Him. Whoever Allah guides, there is no-one who can misguide him, and whoever He

---

2 Reported by Tirmidhī (2485), who classed the hadith as authentic; Ibn Mājah (1334); Aḥmad (451/5); Dārimī (1501); Ibn al-Sunnī (215). Ḥākim (3/13, 4/160) graded the hadith as authentic, and Dhahabī concurred.

misguides, there is no-one who can guide him, and I bear witness that none is worthy of worship except Allah alone, without any partners, and that Muhammad is His slave and Messenger." Ḍimād replied: "Repeat these words to me again, for they have reached the furthest depths of the ocean (i.e., they are the pinnacle of eloquence). Give me your hand so I can pledge my allegiance to you."[3]

Jāmiʿ ibn Shaddād said: "There was a man from among us called Ṭāriq[4] who informed us that he saw the Prophet ﷺ close to Madinah. [The Prophet ﷺ] said to them: 'Do you have anything with you to sell?' We replied: 'We have this camel.' He asked for the price, and we stipulated a certain amount in dates. Afterwards, the Prophet ﷺ took the camel by its saddlebags and proceeded to Madinah. When he had left, we realized that we had sold the camel to a man without knowing his identity. A woman named Ẓaʿīnah, who was with us, said: 'I will serve as guarantor for the price of the camel. I saw the man's face and it was just like the Moon on the night of Badr; it would not disappoint you to witness!'

When we got up in the morning, a man arrived and announced: 'I have been sent by the Messenger of Allah ﷺ; he has instructed you to eat from these dates and to eat until you satisfy yourselves.' So, we did."[5]

There was also the story of al-Julandī, the King of Oman. When the call to Islam reached him from the Messenger of Allah ﷺ, al-Julandī said: "I swear by Allah, I have been shown that this Prophet, who is *ummi*, does not order people to do something good except that he is the first to do it, and neither does he forbid people from something except that he is the first to leave it. When he is victorious, he does not become arrogant,

---

3 Reported by Muslim (868) from the hadith of Ibn ʿAbbās.

4 He was Ṭāriq ibn ʿAbdullāh al-Muḥāribī.

5 Reported by Dāraquṭnī in *Al-Sunan* (3/44-45); Bayhaqī in *Al-Sunan al-Kubrā* (1/76); Ṭabarānī in *Al-Muʿjam al-Kabīr* (8175); Ibn Ḥibbān in *Mawārid al-Ẓamʾān* (1683); and Ḥākim (2/611-612), who was supported by Dhahabī.

and when he is defeated, he does not become despondent. He safeguards any pacts and carries out whatever he has promised. I witness that he is a Prophet!"

Nifṭawayh said that the verse, "...whose oil would almost glow, even without being touched by fire"[6] contained a metaphor for the Prophet ﷺ. His appearance alone, Nifṭawayh said, acts as an evidence of his Prophethood, even without his recitation of the Qur'an. A similar idea was related by the Companion and poet ʿAbdullāh ibn Rawāḥah:

Even if he had not brought clear signs
His appearance would have hinted at the news [that he was sent with].

Prophethood, the Message, and Revelation

Know that if Allah the Almighty wishes to do so, He is fully capable of instilling knowledge in the hearts of those who worship Him, without the need for an intermediary; knowledge of His Essence, His Names, His Characteristics, and all His Capabilities, just as He has mentioned was His way with some of the Prophets. Some of the scholars of Qur'anic exegesis (*tafsīr*) mentioned this point in their explanation of the verse: "It is not possible for a human being to have Allah communicate with them except through inspiration, or from behind a veil, or by sending a Messenger-Angel to reveal what He wills by His permission."[7]

It is also possible for Allah to pass any of this knowledge onto his servants through an intermediary; this intermediary could be other than a human, as with Angels passing on divine revelation to Prophets, or a human, as with Prophets communicating divine revelation to the wider community. There is no intellectual evidence to contradict either scenario.

---

6 *al-Nūr*, 35.

7 *al-Shūrā*, 51.

If this is possible, and we recognize that the Prophets came to mankind with miracles that proved their truthfulness, then it is incumbent upon us to believe them in all matters, because the miracles that Allah bestowed upon the Prophet ﷺ serve as a message from Allah to all human beings; that this is a truthful servant of Mine, so obey him, follow his example, and bear witness to the truthfulness of what he says. This statement is sufficient for now, and whoever wishes to explore the matter further should consult the works of our scholars .

Linguists have differed as to whether the root word for "Prophethood" (*nubuwwah*) contains the letter *hamzah* or not. For those who read it with a *hamzah*, "Prophethood" comes from the same root as the word "news". The meaning of "Prophethood", therefore, is that Allah Exalted has taught a person something from the Unseen and also informed them, or given them the news, that they are a Prophet. In this case, a Prophet takes such a title either by virtue of themselves being foretold, or by virtue of their knowing that Allah Exalted has entrusted them with the mission of Prophethood, and their understanding of the knowledge that Allah has taught them. For those who consider the root to be without the *hamzah*, then the meaning is something that rises from the earth. In the case of Prophets, the implication is that they have an honoured status and lofty rank with their Lord, Most High. In either case, the Prophets are well-deserving of both descriptions combined.

As for the word "Messenger", he is the one who has been sent. His sending is by the order of Allah Exalted, the One who commands him to convey the message to his people. The word "Messenger" also contains the meaning of "succession", evidenced by the saying "the people arrived *having been sent*" (i.e., they arrived in succession, some after the other). It is as if, even from the linguistic root, being a "Messenger" necessitates a consistent repetition of the message you have been sent with. Alternatively, it could express the requirement of the community to always follow the Messenger.

The scholars have differed as to whether the two words "Prophet" and "Messenger" share the same meaning, or have two, distinct meanings. It has been argued that they both come from the root word "foretelling". The proponents of this view use as evidence: "Whenever We sent a Messenger or Prophet before you."[8] They affirm that both words carry the meaning of transmission, and that therefore any Prophet is also a Messenger, and vice versa.

Another view proposes that whilst the two words "Prophet" and "Messenger" overlap in meaning in the sense that they both express being informed of some matters of the Unseen, "Messenger" has the added implication of being sent with a mission to teach and warn others. The supporters of this opinion use the same above-mentioned verse for their argument, maintaining that if "Messenger" and "Prophet" truly shared a single meaning, then it would be more eloquent to express that meaning through a single word, rather than two distinct terms as displayed in the verse. Because of this, they interpret the meaning of the verse as: "We never sent a Messenger [to a people], and neither have We sent a Prophet [who was not sent to inform or educate any specific person]."

A third opinion suggests that a Messenger is someone who brings a set of laws. Otherwise they would be a Prophet, even if they were sent to inform and warn others.

The most correct view – and the one followed by the majority – is that every Messenger is a Prophet, but not every Prophet is a Messenger, and that the first Messenger was Adam, and the final Messenger was our Master Muhammad ﷺ. It was mentioned in the hadith of Abū Dharr that there were 124,000 Prophets, and that 313 of them were Messengers, with the first [of the Messengers] being Adam.[9]

---

8 *al-Ḥajj*, 52.

9 Part of a longer hadith recorded by Bayhaqī in *Al-Sunan* (9/4) and Ibn ʿAdiyy in *Al-Kāmil* (7/2699).

This should clarify the meaning of what it is to be a Prophet or Messenger. According to the experts in this field, there is no specific quality or description that marks someone out as a Prophet. The Karrāmiyyah[10] sect hold such a view, but it is unsubstantiated and unreliable.

As for the word "revelation" (*waḥy*), its root meaning is "to speed up". So, when a Prophet receives what comes to him from his Lord with haste, this is referred to as revelation. Other types of inspiration are also referred to as *waḥy*, due to their similarity to the kind received by a Prophet. Calligraphy can be called *waḥy*, because of the speed of the writer's hand as it moves across the page. The *waḥy* of the eyebrow, and of the glance, is how quickly they can express meaning. Allah Exalted says in the Qur'an, "Signalling to them to glorify Allah morning and evening"[11] meaning, "he indicated", or "he conveyed". From the same root also comes the saying *"al-waḥā, al- waḥā"*, meaning "hurry, hurry!"

Another view suggests that "revelation" carries the root meaning of secrecy and concealment. For this reason, the inspiration or feelings that one finds in the heart can also be termed as *waḥy*. As when Allah Exalted says: "Surely the devils whisper to their human associates to argue with you"[12]; i.e., they whisper in their chests. And when He says: "We inspired the mother of Moses"[13]; i.e., we cast [such a thought] into her heart. This interpretation has also been applied to: "It is not possible for a human being to have Allah communicate with them, except through inspiration…"[14]; i.e., by what He casts into a person's heart, without any intermediary.

Authenticated by Ḥākim (2/597), and Ibn Ḥibbān in *Mawārid al-Ẓam'ān* (94).

10 Founded by the innovator Muhammad ibn Karrām al-Sijistānī, who was an ascetic with little knowledge. He falsely claimed that faith consisted solely of the tongue's enunciation of the Oneness of God, and dismissed the importance of certainty in the heart and actions of the limbs.

11 *Maryam*, 11.

12 *al-An'ām*, 121.

13 *al-Qaṣaṣ*, 7.

14 *al-Shūrā*, 51.

The Miracles of the Prophet ﷺ, and the Meaning of the Word "Miracles"

Actions performed by the Prophets described as miracles are termed as such because humans are otherwise incapable of doing them. There are two types of miracles: the first type is an action that humans are theoretically able to do, but Allah has made impossible for them as a means of confirming the truthfulness of His Prophet ﷺ. Examples of this type of miracle include the disbelievers' refusal to wish for death, and their inability to bring anything resembling the Qur'an.

The second type of miracle are those actions outside of a human's ability. These are miracles that no-one would be able to perform except for Allah. Examples include: bringing the dead back to life; changing the staff into a snake; bringing the female camel out of a rock; the speech of the tree; the gushing of water from the fingers; and the splitting of the Moon. Allah performs these miracles at the hand of His Prophet ﷺ and, to prove the incapacity of those who disbelieve in the Prophet ﷺ, He challenges them to produce something similar.

The miracles performed by the Prophet ﷺ consisted of both types: those that humans are prevented from doing, and those outside their capabilities. These miracles both confirmed his Prophethood and proved his honesty. Out of all the Prophets, the final Messenger ﷺ was sent with the greatest number of miracles, the most magnificent signs, and the clearest proofs. The miracles of the Prophet ﷺ were innumerable. In fact, if we chose just one of those miracles, namely the Qur'an, you would never be able to count the thousands of extraordinary signs contained within it. Even when the Prophet ﷺ set a challenge to replicate one surah from the Qur'an, none of his detractors were able to do so.

Scholars have added that even the shortest surah – "We have given you plenty"[15] – is absolutely inimitable. Therefore, we can say that each and every verse of the Qur'an is a miraculous sign.

The miracles of the Prophet ﷺ fall into two categories. The first category contains those miracles that are undisputedly authentic and have been transmitted to us through numerous, concurring chains of narration, like the Qur'an. For these miracles, there is absolutely no controversy, difference of opinion, or doubt that the Prophet ﷺ performed them and used them as evidence. If the most stubborn disbeliever wanted to deny that they happened, it would be as far-fetched as denying that the Prophet ﷺ lived in this world. The very existence of the Qur'an proves them wrong; it is, without doubt, miraculous, and so is everything it contains.

As the scholars have commented, there is a general principle to be applied: if one miracle that the Prophet ﷺ performed does not reach the level of undisputed authenticity in isolation, then the plethora of miracles taken as a whole certainly do. Neither believers nor disbelievers differ as to whether the Prophet ﷺ performed these miracles. Even the most persistent detractors take issue not with their occurrence, but with the fact that they were from Allah. As aforementioned, the miracles certainly were from Allah, and they are a confirmation of His words to His Prophet ﷺ: "You have told the truth."

Another way we can be certain that the Prophet ﷺ performed these miracles is by the consistency of the reports describing their occurrence. In the same vein, it is well-known that Ḥātim was generous, that ʿAntarah was brave, and that al-Aḥnaf ibn Qays was patient; although a single report of generosity, bravery, or patience would not necessarily prove it to be fact, a multitude of consistent reports makes it common knowledge.

The second category of the miracles of the Prophet ﷺ contains those miracles that do not reach the level of undisputed authenticity, and this

---

15 *al-Kawthar*, 1.

category can also be divided into two types. The first type are those miracles that are very well-known, and transmitted through numerous chains of narration. These have been widely reported by the scholars of hadith and Sīrah (the study of the life of the Prophet ﷺ); for example, the gushing of water from between the fingers, and the story of a small amount of food miraculously feeding many.

The second type within this category are only related by one or two people, and are transmitted through fewer chains of narration than those mentioned above. However, they can be combined with other narrations that agree in meaning, and also contribute to the over-arching body of evidence for the miracles of the Prophet ﷺ. The author would add that, in reality, many of the miracles attributed to the Prophet ﷺ can be confirmed with undisputed authenticity.

Let us take the example of the splitting of the Moon. Firstly, it is clearly stated within the Qur'an. In this instance, there is no reason for us to deviate from the literal meaning of the text without a documented proof to support doing so. Furthermore, the splitting of the Moon was confirmed in authentic and sound reports, which have been transmitted to us through many different chains of narration. And because there is so much evidence that the event took place, we are not going to have our firmness of certainty weakened by the differing of foolish people, who are themselves completely void of religious morals. Neither will we succumb to the absurd accusations of the ones who innovate matters in the religion; they are just trying to sow doubts in the hearts of weak believers! Instead, we are going to completely reject their arguments, throw their words back in their faces, and leave them out in the cold.

Similarly, the stories of gushing water from between his fingers, and the small amount of food that kept increasing, have both been reported by a great number of reliable narrators of hadith, including many of the Companions.

Some miracles have been reported with a direct chain of transmission from the Companions. This includes occasions when a great number of the Companions had gathered, such as at the Battle of the Trench, the Patrol of Buwāṭ[16], the minor pilgrimage (*'umrah*) of Ḥudaybiyyah[17], the Battle of Tabūk[18], and other times when the Muslim community had gathered together, or their armies had assembled.

Not a single one of the Companions contradicted or objected to the descriptions of the miracles when they heard them, or contested the statements attributed to them; in this case, the silence of the Companions is just as if they had spoken up in agreement, because they would never remain silent if they heard something false, nor would they lie in order to save face or gain favour. No wish nor fear would prevent them from sticking to the truth. In fact, if a Companion heard something which was unknown to them, they would reject it, even if another Companion had reported it as being from the practices (Sunnah) or the life (Sīrah) of the Prophet ﷺ, or from the modes of recitation of the Qur'an. There were times when some Companions would say that other Companions had made a mistake or had misunderstood a particular issue. All this connects back to the central point that – as we have made clear – the miracles of the Prophet ﷺ certainly took place.

Also, any examples of hadith or reported events which have no authentic origin, or are built on falsehood, will undoubtedly be exposed as such. This will be done through both the passage of time and the efforts of those who investigate hadith in order to distinguish those that are fab-

---

16 The Prophet ﷺ had gone to Buwāṭ, in the second year after the *hijrah*, with the intention of intercepting a caravan of the Quraysh on its return journey from Syria, but they took a different route. Buwāṭ was located by Mount Juhaynah, on the route from Madinah towards the port of Yanbū'.

17 Also known as the Battle of Ḥudaybiyyah. Ḥudaybiyyah is located 22 kilometres east of Makkah, on the route towards Jeddah.

18 The battle took place in the ninth year after the *hijrah*. Tābūk is a city located 778 kilometres north of Madinah.

ricated or weak. This can be seen with several false or obscure reports which were subsequently identified as such. The signs of our Prophet ﷺ, however, only become clearer and more convincing with the passage of time. This is despite a plethora of sects that have come and gone, numerous attacks by enemies of the religion hell-bent on undermining and refuting the authenticity of these miracles. These people are filled with rage and resentment. Even when faced with atheists determined to extinguish their beauty, the miracles of the Prophet ﷺ continue to increase in their potency and acceptance.

The same can be said of his reports about the Unseen, and his foretelling of future events. The signs the Prophet ﷺ was sent with are well-known; this is a truth that cannot be covered up. This was confirmed by esteemed scholars including Abū Bakr al-Bāqillānī, Abū Bakr ibn Fūrak, and others . Anyone claiming that these famous stories have only been reported from one source have either not spent the time to read all the material, or have been caught up with studying other sciences. Those who have properly analysed the relevant hadith and chains of transmission would not make such statements, for all the reasons we have outlined above. It is not far-fetched for one person to take knowledge on a matter from many sources, whilst another has no knowledge of it whatsoever. Let us take the example of Baghdad; most people know that it exists, that it is a great city, and the home of the Emirate and the Caliphate, and yet many others do not even know the name of the place, let alone anything about it. Likewise, the scholars of jurisprudence from the companions of Imam Mālik know, through many complementary reports and without needing to elaborate, that their school of thought (*madhhab*) requires both the Imam and the congregation to read Surah al-Fātiḥah during prayer, and allows making an intention to fast on the first night of Ramadan to suffice for the whole month. Imam al-Shāfiʿī believed that the intention had to be renewed on each night of Ramadan, and allowed wiping over only a part of the head during ablutions (*wuḍū'*). Both schools of thought observe the law of retaliation (*qiṣāṣ*) for murder; require an intention to be made before *wuḍū'*; and stipulate a legal guardian (*walī*) for the female partner as a pre-condition for the marriage contract. Abū Ḥanīfah, on the other hand, has different rulings on these matters. There are people who do not know the opinions and rulings of their own school of thought, let alone others.

The Miraculous Nature of the Qur'an

Understand – and may Allah help us – that many aspects of the Mighty Book of Allah are of a miraculous nature. In order to accurately compile these features, we have arranged them into four categories.

The first category concerns the beauty of the cohesion of the Qur'an, the harmony of its word structure, and the purity of its Arabic language. The rhetoric of the Qur'an is part of its miraculous nature, as it far outstripped the literary customs of the Arabs at that time, despite notoriety for their mastery of the field.

The Arabs were exemplary in linguistic expression, having been gifted with an eloquence of tongue and wisdom in speech unlike any other nation. They were given a fluency of expression no other people possessed, and a clarity of oration which delved straight to the heart of a matter. Allah made this a part of their nature and habit. The Arabs would amaze people with their skills of improvisation, and had an ability to find the right turn of phrase for any situation. Through the power of their speech – oscillating between appeal and reproach, lavishing praise and cutting condemnation – the Arabs would implore and reach out, and had the ability to raise some in ranks, whilst bringing others crashing to the ground. Their words worked a type of magic that was permissible, and they could arrange a sequence of adjectives more beautiful than a string of pearls. The Arabs used language to trick intelligent people; to overcome difficulties; to heal or reignite long-standing feuds; to make cowards brave; to open the hands of the tight-fisted (i.e., to make stingy people generous); and to render the imperfect as perfect, and the one who was once nimble and intelligent as lazy and sluggish.

From the Arabs, the Bedouins in particular were known for concise and refined speech, a majestic command of the language, as well as strong, outgoing personality and a pure, disarming nature. On the other hand, the people from the cities were known for their skillful rhetoric, decisive discourse, and concise and comprehensive speech, alongside an easygoing manner and ability to express beauty and kindness in a few gentle words.

Both groups possessed an eloquence of profound language, never failing to find the precise phrase to win any argument and open any path, like a piercing dart. They never doubted themselves and were exact in their choice of words. As true masters of Arabic, they took ownership of their speech and had discovered the springs of knowledge. They had studied the science from every possible angle and used their proficiency to construct literary masterpieces, like lofty towers of gold, reaching towards the sky. They spoke on all matters; both the great and the menial, the weighty and the insignificant. Either sparing or verbose depending on the conversation, the Arabs were equally confident in poetry and prose.

No-one could have amazed these people except a Noble Messenger with a Mighty Book: "It cannot be proven false from any angle. It is a revelation from the One Who is All-Wise, Praiseworthy."[19] Every verse is precise and exact, and every word is detailed and clear. This is a book that mesmerizes the intellect, in a pure Arabic that overcomes any other speech and unites brevity and inimitability. Both the literal and the metaphorical are clarified and articulated. As you read the text, each section competes in beauty with the next. Its conciseness complements the beauty of its structure, and the choice of words convey many layers

---

19 *Fuṣṣilat*, 42.

of meaning.

The Arabs were the most proficient in the field of linguistics by miles. They had the most famous orators; the greatest improvisers in poetry and rhyme; and the most comprehensive in their knowledge of unusual expressions, which they confidently used both for everyday conversation and fiery debate. These are the people that the Prophet ﷺ was calling out to for just over twenty years, challenging and rebuking them, and not sparing a single moment to invite them to the religion of Allah.

"Or do they claim 'He made it up'? Tell them O Prophet, 'Produce one surah like it then, and seek help from whoever you can – other than Allah – if what you say is true!'"[20]

"And if you are in doubt about what We have revealed to Our servant, then produce a surah like it and call your helpers other than Allah, if what you say is true. But if you are unable to do so – and you will never be able to do so – then fear the Fire fuelled with people and stones, which is prepared for the disbelievers."[21]

"Say, O Prophet, 'If all humans and jinn were to come together to produce the equivalent of this Qur'an, they could not produce its equal, no matter how they supported each other.'"[22]

"Say, O Prophet, 'Produce ten fabricated surahs like it and seek help from whoever you can – other than Allah – if what you say is true.'"[23]

The Prophet ﷺ continued to chastise the Arabs with robust condemnation, and reprimand them in the strongest possible terms. He would undermine their claims to knowledge and humble their leaders. The social order that had become entrenched was thoroughly shattered. He

---

20 *Yūnus*, 38.

21 *al-Baqarah*, 23-24.

22 *al-Isrā'*, 88.

23 *Hūd*, 13.

devalued their false idols and denounced the corrupt ways of their ancestors. Their land, property, and wealth were confiscated. Despite all this, they were reluctant to respond to the challenge posed in the Qur'an, and continued to be unable to produce anything like it. Instead, they relied on stirring trouble amongst their own ranks through self-delusion, false rumours, and incitement. They would lie to one another about the Qur'an, saying: "This Qur'an is nothing but magic from the ancients",[24] "same old magic",[25] "a fabrication which he made up with the help of others",[26] and "ancient fables".[27]

They would make shocking, false statements, and had no interest in matters pertaining to the Hereafter, with excuses including "our hearts are unreceptive",[28] "our hearts are veiled against what you are calling us to, there is deafness in our ears, and there is a barrier between us and you",[29] and instructing their followers "Do not listen to this Qur'an but drown it out so that you may prevail."[30]

The enemies of the religion presumed that they would be able to imitate the Qur'an, and they said: "If we wanted, we could have easily produced something similar"[31], but Allah Exalted informed them, "...you will never be able to do so".[32] Of course, they were never able to do so. For any foolish person that tried, like Musaylamah the Liar, Allah would expose their shortcomings for all to see and strip them of their pomp; the

---

24 *al-Muddaththir*, 24.

25 *al-Qamar*, 2.

26 *al-Furqān*, 4.

27 *al-An'ām*, 25.

28 *al-Baqarah*, 88.

29 *Fuṣṣilat*, 5.

30 *Fuṣṣilat*, 26.

31 *al-Anfāl*, 31.

32 *al-Baqarah*, 24.

delicate speech they used to mislead others. Otherwise, the intelligent people amongst them may not have realized that the Qur'an was nothing like the eloquence or rhetoric of men. Instead, the ones who heard the Qur'an were in awe, either guided by its message or, at least, captivated by its beauty.

Al-Walīd ibn al-Mughīrah heard the Prophet ﷺ reciting: "Indeed, Allah commands justice, grace, as well as courtesy to close relatives. He forbids indecency, wickedness, and aggression. He instructs you so perhaps you will be mindful."[33] He responded: "I swear by Allah, this [Qur'an] has a sweetness to it...No human could have come up with this!"[34]

Abū ʿUbayd al-Qāsim ibn Salām mentions that a Bedouin man heard someone reciting: "So proclaim what you have been commanded, and turn away from the polytheists"[35] so he immediately fell into prostration. He said: "I prostrated because of the beauty of its language." On a separate occasion, another Bedouin heard someone reciting: "When they lost all hope in him, they spoke privately"[36] He responded: "I bear witness that no-one would be able to produce this type of speech."

It is said that one day, ʿUmar ibn al-Khaṭṭāb was sleeping in the mosque, when suddenly he found someone standing next to his head, testifying to the truth. He questioned him, and the man informed ʿUmar that he was one of the Byzantine generals, and that he was well-versed in Arabic and other languages. He also said that he had heard one of the Muslim prisoners of war reciting verses from the Qur'an. "Upon reflection", the man added, "I realized that this book contained the same descriptions of this life and the Hereafter as that which was revealed to ʿĪsā ibn Maryam."

---

33 *al-Naḥl,* 90.

34 Related by Bayhaqī in *Al-Manāhil*, p. 518 from the hadith of ʿIkrimah; and ʿIrāqī in *Takhrīj Aḥādīth al-Iḥyā'* (1/274); and it was graded as authentic by Ḥākim (2/506-507), and Dhahabī concurred.

35 *al-Ḥijr,* 94.

36 *Yūsuf,* 80.

He was referring to the words of Allah Exalted: "For whoever obeys Allah and His Messenger, and fears Allah and is mindful of Him, then it is they who will truly triumph."[37]

It was related from ʿAbd al-Malik ibn Qurayb al-Aṣmaʿī that he once heard a slave-girl speaking, so he said to her: "Incredible! Where did you learn such eloquent speech?" She replied: "How can we describe my words as eloquence, after hearing the words of Allah, when He said, 'We inspired the mother of Moses: "Nurse him, but when you fear for him, put him then into the river, and do not grieve. We will certainly return him to you, and make him one of the Messengers."'[38] In a single verse, He has combined two commands, two prohibitions, two pieces of information and two pieces of good news!"

This aspect of the miraculous nature of the Qur'an is unique to it, and is built on two pieces of evidence. The fact that the Qur'an was communicated to us by the Prophet ﷺ is well-known and undisputed. Similarly, it is well known that the Prophet ﷺ presented the Qur'an as a challenge, and that the Arabs were unable to imitate it. No-one denies either that the eloquence of the Qur'an was beyond the scope of the linguistic and literary habits of the time; this was attested to by the Arabs, the very people who knew the language best. As for those not so well-versed in the field, their way of finding out about the miraculous nature of the eloquence of the Qur'an was by the confirmation of those who had mastered the Arabic language, and their incapability to bring anything like it.

Alternatively, one could simply ponder the meaning of the words of Allah Exalted:

"There is security of life for you in the law of retaliation"[39]; "If only

---

37 *al-Nūr*, 52.

38 *al-Qaṣaṣ*, 7.

39 *al-Baqarah*, 179.

you could see when they will be horrified with no escape on Judgement Day! And they will be seized from a nearby place."[40]; "Respond to evil with what is best, then the one you are in a feud with will be like a close friend."[41]

"And it was said, 'O earth, swallow up your water,' and 'O sky, withhold your rain.' The floodwater receded and the decree was carried out. The Ark rested on al-Jūdī, and it was said: 'Away with the wrongdoing people.'"[42]; "So We seized each people for their sin: against some of them We sent a storm of stones, some were overtaken by a mighty blast, some We caused the earth to swallow, and some We drowned."[43]

There are many verses like these. In fact, the majority of the Qur'an could be mentioned above. We have detailed the conciseness of the Qur'an's language, the many layers of meaning, the clarity of expression, the beauty of its structure and composition, and the perfection of its lexicon. Every word in the Qur'an could fill volumes of contemplation, and behind every phrase lies an ocean of meaning. Despite a proliferation of texts, just some of the benefits to be taken and deductions to be made from this Mighty Book have been investigated.

The style of the Qur'an includes lengthy stories, interwoven with tales of past generations. In other circumstances, the people of rhetoric would have considered this as linguistically deficient. However, the one who truly reflects in the context of the Qur'an will notice the perfection in the links from one story to the next, and the symmetry of the cohesive narrative; as with the story of the Prophet Yūsūf, told in its entirety.

Each time these stories are repeated in different places in the Qur'an,

---

40 *Saba'*, 51.

41 *Fuṣṣilat*, 34.

42 *Hūd*, 44.

43 *al-'Ankabūt*, 40

they are told with an array of imagery and description, until each mention of an event appears as if it is the first. This variety of expression is part of the beauty of the Qur'an; the soul never tires from its repetition, and the heart shows no hostility to hearing its stories again.

The Style and Coherence of the Qur'an

The second aspect of the miraculous nature of the Qur'an is its perfect order and harmonious coherence. The literary style of the Qur'an was completely unique, and did not resemble anything the Arabs had authored. It was completely different from their methods of composing poetry or prose. In the Qur'an, the division of the verses cause the reciter to pause, whilst the meaning of the words continue into the next. Nothing like this had been seen before, or would be seen after, and no-one was able to replicate this distinctive style. They raged and exhausted their intellectual capacities trying to comprehend what they had heard, but were left bewildered. No-one was inspired to write something like it from any of the literary genres at their disposal; neither prose, rhyme, nor any type of poetry could come to their rescue.

When al-Walīd ibn al-Mughīrah heard the Prophet ﷺ reciting the Qur'an, his heart began to soften. Upon hearing this, Abū Jahl arrived to remonstrate. Al-Walīd stood his ground, declaring: "I swear by Allah, I know more about poetry than any of you! I swear by Allah, what he just recited does not resemble any type of poetry!"[44]

In another report from al-Walīd ibn al-Mughīrah,[45] he mentions one of the seasonal gatherings of the Quraysh, when he said: "The delegations of the Arabs are due to arrive shortly, so let us agree on an opinion

---

44 Reported by Ḥākim (2/506-507), Bayhaqī in *Al-Dalā'il*, and al-Wāḥidī in *Asbāb al-Nuzūl* (330) from the hadith of Ibn ʿAbbās. Ḥākim graded the hadith as authentic, and Dhahabī concurred.

45 Reported by Ibn Isḥāq in *Al-Sīrah* (150-151) from the hadith of Ibn ʿAbbās.

about him (i.e., the Prophet ﷺ) so that we do not contradict each other." They responded: "Let us say that he is a fortune-teller." Al-Walīd replied: "I swear by Allah, he is not a fortune-teller. Neither is he a person who mutters under his breath or recites poetry." They said: "In that case, let us say that he is insane." Al-Walīd replied: "He is not insane, neither is he possessed by a jinn or listening to their whispers." They said: "In that case, let us say that he is a poet." Al-Walīd replied: "He is not a poet. We are already well-versed in all the genres and meters of poetry, and this man is not a poet." So, they said: "Let us say that he is a magician." Al-Walīd replied: "He is not a magician. He does not follow their practices of tying knots and blowing on them." Finally, the people asked: "What shall we say then?" Al-Walīd replied: "Every single claim you have made, I know to be false. The closest you have come to the truth is saying he is a magician, because black magic can separate a man from his father, his brother, his wife, and his tribe."

The people departed and sat down on the paths to warn those who were arriving. Allah revealed, regarding al-Walīd: "Leave Me to him whom I created alone. And gave him vast wealth. And children as witnesses. And smoothed things for him. Then he wants Me to add yet more! By no means! He was stubborn towards Our revelations. I will exhaust him increasingly. He thought and analyzed. May he perish, how he analyzed. Again: may he perish, how he analyzed. Then he looked, then he frowned and whined. Then he turned back and was proud. And said, 'This Qur'an is nothing but magic from the ancients.'"[46]

When ʿUtbah ibn Rabīʿah[47] heard the Qur'an, he said: "My people! You know that I do not leave anything without learning, reading, and speaking

---

46 *Muddaththir*, 24.

47 He was ʿUtbah ibn Rabīʿah ibn ʿAbd Shams, one of the leaders of the Quraysh during the times of ignorance. He was killed at the Battle of Badr and died as a disbeliever.

about it. I swear by Allah, I have heard a particular type of speech and I swear by Allah, I have never heard anything like it. It is not poetry, or black magic, or fortune-telling."[48] Al-Naḍr ibn al-Ḥārith said something similar.

In the hadith about Abū Dharr embracing Islam, he describes his brother Unays: "I swear by Allah, I have not heard of anyone more proficient in poetry than my brother Unays. He contested with twelve poets during the times of ignorance, and I was one of them. Unays continued on to Makkah, and returned to me with news about the Prophet ﷺ. I asked: 'What do the people say about him?' Unays replied: 'They say that he is a poet, a fortune-teller, and a magician. However, I have heard the words of fortune-tellers, and he is not one of them. I have compared his speech with all types of poetry and rhyme, and it does not match up. No-one should come after me and claim that he is a poet. He is the truthful one, and they are the liars.'"[49]

The hadiths on this topic are authentic and numerous. The Qur'an has a miraculous nature from two standpoints: in terms of its brevity and eloquence, and in terms of its unique literary style. Upon scrutiny, both are aspects of its inimitability, and the Arabs were unable to replicate either feature. It was completely beyond their powers. The Qur'an stood in stark contrast to the words and speech of the Arabs of the time, as confirmed by the investigations of several leading scholars in the field. Some who came after them tried to argue that the miraculous nature of the Qur'an was simply a sum of its eloquence and style; such a statement should cause the listener to recoil, and a sound heart to reject. The correct opinion is the one we have presented above, which is shared by the masters of rhetoric.

---

48 Reported by Bayhaqī, from the hadith of Muhammad ibn Ka'b. Also mentioned in *Al-Sīrah* of Ibn Kathīr (1/503).

49 Reported by Muslim (2473). See also Bukhārī (3861).

Knowledge of these matters is both imperative and unambiguous.

What the scholars of the people of the Sunnah have disagreed about is precisely which aspect of the Qur'an people were unable to replicate. The majority propose that the inimitability of the Qur'an is comprised in the power of its clear and lucid expression, alongside its perfected structure, concise speech, and unique composition and literary style, all of which are outside the scope of a human's capabilities. By this argument, the Qur'an is miraculous in the sense that it would not be possible, even theoretically, for a human to reproduce it, just like the miracles of bringing the dead back to life, the transformation of the staff, and the pebbles that were given the ability to praise Allah.

Abū al-Ḥasan al-Ashʿarī, on the other hand, took the view that whilst it would theoretically be possible for a human being to imitate the Qur'an, it has not happened and will not happen, because Allah has prevented us from doing so. A number of scholars concurred with this opinion. It has already been established that the Arabs were unable to replicate the Qur'an, but it would have been unfair to use this as an argument and a proof against them, if it was something outside of a human being's physical capabilities to begin with. However, they were challenged to bring something like it, and they failed. Without the justification of the task lying outside the realms of possibility, their failures are an even more powerful evidence against them.

In any case, the Arabs could not come up with one line. Instead, they suffered many losses in battle, and were forced to abandon their city and their wealth. Having been a people who arrogantly held their heads aloft, they now tasted humiliation. They had not willingly chosen such a fate, but were forcibly disgraced. The alternative would have been far easier; to imitate the Qur'an – had it been within their capability – would have led to a swift success, a definitive response to the challenge they had been set, and a resounding victory over their adversaries.

The Arabs, above all people, were powerful linguists. Every one of them tried his utmost to obscure the beauty and extinguish the light of the Qur'an, but their struggles were to no avail. They desperately searched for some inner reserves, but there was no use. Despite their great numbers, aiding and abetting one another over a prolonged period, they could not utter a single word. They were prevented in their mission and found themselves cut off at every turn.

Reports of Unseen Events in the Qur'an

Reports of things that were unseen and accurate predictions of events that had not yet occurred are the third feature of the Qur'an's miraculous nature. The examples of this are many:

After the Treaty of Ḥudaybiyyah: "Allah willing, you will surely enter the Sacred Mosque, in security."[50]

Regarding the Romans: "Yet following their defeat, they will triumph."[51]

For the believers: "Allah has promised those of you who believe and do good that He will certainly make them successors in the land, as He did with those before them; and He will surely establish for them their faith which He has chosen for them; and will indeed change their fear into security – provided that they worship Me, associating nothing with Me. But whoever disbelieves after this promise, it is they who will be the rebellious."[52]

"When Allah's ultimate help comes and the victory over Mecca is achieved, and you – O Prophet – see the people embracing Allah's Way in crowds, then glorify the praises of your Lord and seek His Forgiveness, for certainly He is Ever-Accepting of Repentance."[53]

---

50 *al-Fatḥ*, 27.

51 *al-Rūm*, 3.

52 *al-Nūr*, 55.

53 *al-Naṣr*, 1-3.

All of these events took place, just as Allah Exalted said they would. The Romans defeated the Persians within a few years, and people entered the religion of Islam in droves. By the time the Prophet ﷺ died, Islam had spread across the entire Arab world.

Allah made the believers successful, strengthened their religion, and bestowed upon them authority across the world, from east to west, just as the Prophet ﷺ had said: "The Earth was gathered before me, and I was shown its east and its west. The sovereignty of my nation will reach as far as that which was gathered before me."[54]

Allah Exalted says in the Qur'an: "It is certainly We Who have revealed the Reminder, and it is certainly We Who will preserve it",[55] and this has been the case. So many have tried to change its words and alter its rulings. Countless groups of atheists, deniers of the attributes of Allah, and especially the Qarmatians[56], have been combining their efforts, plans and strength; up till now, they have been doing this for five hundred years.[57] Nevertheless, they have failed to extinguish a scintilla of the light of the Qur'an. They have been unable to change a single word, or to make the Muslims doubt a single letter. Praise be to Allah!

There are many other accurate predictions made in the Qur'an:

"Soon their united front will be defeated and forced to flee."[58] "So fight them and Allah will punish them at your hands, put them to shame, help you overcome them, and soothe the hearts of the believers."[59] "He is the One Who has sent His Messenger with true guidance and the religion of

---

54 Reported by Muslim (2889) from the hadith of Thawbān.

55 *al-Ḥijr*, 9.

56 A group from the Bāṭiniyyah (Ismaili Shia) sect, who take their name from their founder – either known as Ḥamdān, or al-Faraj ibn ʿUthmān, or al-Faraj ibn Yaḥyā – who took the nickname Qirmiṭ.

57 This was at the time the book was first published.

58 *al-Qamar*, 45.

59 *al-Tawbah*, 14.

truth, making it prevail over all others, even to the dismay of polytheists."[60] "They can never inflict harm on you, except a little annoyance. But if they meet you in battle, they will flee and they will have no helpers."[61]

All these things took place just as Allah Exalted said they would. Another way He comments on unseen events in the Qur'an is by exposing the secrets of the Hypocrites and the Jews, and shedding light on the lies and conversations they would share in private:

"...and they say to one another, 'Why does Allah not punish us for what we say?'"[62] "They conceal in their hearts what they do not reveal to you. They say to themselves, 'If we had any say in the matter, none of us would have come to die here.' Say, O Prophet, 'Even if you were to remain in your homes, those among you who were destined to be killed would have been met with the same fate.' Though this, Allah tests what is within you and purifies what is in your hearts. And Allah knows best what is hidden in the heart."[63]

"...nor those among the Jews who eagerly listen to lies, attentive to those who are too arrogant to come to you. They distort the Scripture, taking rulings out of context, then say, 'If this is the ruling you get from Muhammad, accept it. If not, beware!' Whoever Allah allows to be deluded, you can never be of any help to them against Allah. It is not Allah's Will to purify their hearts. For them is disgrace in this world, and they will suffer a tremendous punishment in the hereafter."[64] "Some Jews take words out of context and say, 'We listen and we disobey', 'Hear! May you never hear', and '*Rā'inā* (herd us)' – playing with words and discrediting the faith."[65]

---

60 *al-Tawbah*, 33.

61 Āl ʿImrān, 111.

62 *al-Mujādilah*, 8.

63 Āl ʿImrān, 154.

64 *al-Mā'idah*, 41.

65 *al-Nisā'*, 46.

Allah said, confirming the guarantee He made to His Prophet ﷺ and what the Muslims had wished for on the day of Badr: "Remember, O believers, when Allah promised to give you the upper hand over either target, you wish to capture the unarmed party."[66]

When Allah Exalted revealed: "Surely We will be sufficient for you against the mockers"[67], the Prophet ﷺ congratulated his Companions with the news that Allah would suffice them. The "mockers" referred to in the verse were a group in Makkah who were trying to harm the Prophet ﷺ and turning people away from him. They were destroyed. As Allah said: "Allah will certainly protect you from the people."[68] This was evident in the case of the people who wished for the Prophet ﷺ to be harmed and intended to kill him, and the reports confirming this are authentic and well-known.

Stories of Previous Nations in the Qur'an

The fourth feature of the miraculous nature of the Qur'an is contained in its descriptions of past generations, vanquished empires, and previous systems of law. These were stories that Jewish and Christian scholars had dedicated their entire lives to uncovering, but only came up with one piece of the puzzle. The Prophet ﷺ brought this information in the correct manner and with authentic texts, until the people of knowledge had to confirm the accuracy and truth of what had been revealed, and that it could not have been learnt through study alone. They already knew that the Prophet ﷺ was *ummi*. Neither was he engaged in intense study or research. The Prophet ﷺ did not frequently remain absent from the people around him, so no-one was unaware of his circumstances.

---

66 *al-Anfāl*, 7.

67 *al-Ḥijr*, 95.

68 *al-Mā'idah*, 67.

The People of the Book[69] used to ask the Prophet ﷺ a lot about these matters, so he would recite to them from the Qur'an that which had been revealed to him. He recited about previous Prophets and their nations, the stories of Mūsā and al-Khiḍr, Yūsuf and his brothers, the People of the Cave, Dhū al-Qarnayn, Luqmān and his son, and other stories. He also recited to them from passages describing the beginning of creation, and mentioning what was contained in the Torah, the Gospel, the Psalms of Dāwūd, and the Pages revealed to Ibrāhīm and Mūsā. The scholars confirmed the accuracy of what he read to them. They could not lie about what had been revealed, and had no option but to yield to the truth. So, whomever Allah facilitated, believed in the goodness that had come to them, and whoever was destined for evil remained stubborn and jealous.

There are no reports of the Jews and the Christians denying what had been revealed in the Qur'an. This was despite their intense enmity towards the Prophet ﷺ, their determination for people to deny him, and their lengthy remonstrations and protests against him with what their own books contained. They questioned the Prophet ﷺ and would demand to hear the secrets of their academic sciences, contents of their biographies, information about what had been hidden from their books and laws, and stories of their Prophets. They asked about the Spirit, Dhū al-Qarnayn, the People of the Cave, ʿĪsā, the law of stoning, what Isrā'īl[70] forbade himself, and which cattle and wholesome foods that had previously been permissible became forbidden to them because of their outrageous behaviour. As Allah mentions: "This is their description in the Torah. And their parable in the Gospel is that of a seed that sprouts its tiny branches, making it strong. Then it becomes thick, standing firmly on its stern, to the delight

69 i.e., the Jews and the Christians.

70 Another name for Prophet Yaʿqūb.

of the planters."[71]

There were other matters that they would ask about, and the Prophet ﷺ would answer them and inform them from whatever had been revealed to him in the Qur'an. There is no evidence of them denying what he brought. Rather, the majority of them confirmed the fact that he was a Prophet, and declared the truthfulness of what he said. Indeed, many were aware of their own stubbornness and envy, like the people of Najrān[72], Ibn Ṣūriyā[73], the two sons of Akhṭab[74], and others.

Anyone who continued to fabricate material, bragging that what they possessed contradicted that which had been revealed to the Prophet ﷺ, was called to bring their proof, and their claims were exposed as false. It was said to them: "'Bring the Torah and read it, if your claims are true.' Then whoever still fabricates lies about Allah, they will be the true wrongdoers."[75] They were reprimanded for doing so. Whoever admitted the impertinence and audacity of their claims was shown how scandalous his actions were by the book in his own hand.[76]

There are no reports of the Jews or the Christians bringing anything from their books to contradict the Qur'an, either from authentic or weak sources. As Allah Exalted says: "O People of the Book! Now our Messenger has come to you, revealing much of what you have hidden of the Scriptures and disregarding much. There certainly has come to you from

---

71 *al-Fatḥ*, 29.

72 Najrān was an ancient city located 910 kilometes southeast of Makkah. It was inhabited by a Christian tribe whom the Prophet ﷺ called to *al-mubālah*, a type of supplication where two parties pray that Allah curses whichever of them is the oppressor, but had declined out of fear.

73 Abdullāh ibn Ṣūriyā, a Jewish rabbi who once attempted to conceal the verse of stoning in the Torah by placing his hand over it whilst reading aloud, as mentioned in Bukhārī (6841) and Muslim (1699).

74 They are Ḥuyayy ibn Akhṭab al-Yahūdī and his brother Abū Yāsir.

75 *Āl ʿImrān*, 93-94.

76 An apparent reference to Abdullāh ibn Ṣūriyā.

Allah a light and clear Book through which Allah guides those who seek His pleasure to the ways of peace, brings them out of darkness and into light by His Will, and guides them to the Straight Path."[77]

Challenges in the Qur'an to the People of the Book, and Their Inability to Respond

These four features of the Qur'an's miraculous nature are crystal clear; there is no contention or doubt about them. Another aspect of its inimitability are the verses which declared people's inability to answer certain challenges. For example, Allah addresses the Jews: "Say, O Prophet, 'If the eternal Home of the Hereafter with Allah is exclusively for you Israelites out of all humanity, then wish for death if what you say is true!' But they will never wish for that because of what their hands have done. And Allah has perfect knowledge of the wrongdoers."[78] Abū Isḥāq al-Zajjāj said: "This verse is the strongest proof and the clearest evidence of the authenticity of the Message, because whilst Allah Exalted said 'then wish for death', he informed the Jews that they never would, and subsequently not one of them did."

The Prophet ﷺ said: "I swear by the one in whose hand is my soul, no man from them could say that without choking on his spit"[79] i.e., dying there and then. Allah turned the Jews away from wishing for death and made them fear it in order to affirm the truth of His Messenger ﷺ and the accuracy of His revelation. If the Jews had any power to wish for death just to prove the Prophet ﷺ wrong, they would have made sure to do so; rather, it is Allah Exalted who does whatever He wishes.

---

77 *al-Mā'idah*, 15-16.

78 *al-Baqarah*, 94-95.

79 Reported by Bayhaqī in *Al-Dalā'il* from the hadith of Ibn ʿAbbās. See also Aḥmad (1/248), and Suyūṭī in *Al-Manāhil*, p. 527.

Abū Muhammad al-Aṣīlī[80] said: "The strangest thing is that from the day Allah Exalted ordered His Prophet ﷺ to say this, not a single individual or group from amongst the Jews ever confronted him or answered back to him again." The verse remained as an evidence against anyone from amongst them who felt that they could test the Prophet ﷺ.

It was the same with the verse of the mutual curse. When the bishops of Najrān came to the Prophet ﷺ, Allah Exalted revealed: "Now, whoever disputes with you O Prophet concerning Jesus after full knowledge has come to you, say, 'Come! Let us gather our children and your children, our women and your women, ourselves and yourselves – then let us sincerely invoke Allah's curse upon the liars.'[81]"[82] The bishops refrained from accepting the proposition, preferring to pay the jizyah tax instead. That was because their leader, al-ʿĀqib[83], said to them: "You know that he is a Prophet, and when a Prophet curses a people, it does not spare either the great or weak amongst them."

Allah also promised: "And if you are in doubt about what We have revealed to Our servant, then produce a surah like it and call your helpers other than Allah if what you say is true."[84] He informed the Arabs that they would not be able to replicate the Qur'an, and so was the case.

The Feeling of Fear Upon Hearing the Qur'an

Also from the miraculous nature of the Qur'an is the fear that clings

---

80 He was ʿAbdullāh ibn Ibrāhīm al-Aṣīlī, taking his name from the town of Aṣīlah in Morocco. He was a great scholar of the Mālikī *madhhab*, and an expert in deciphering weaknesses in hadiths and investigating the biographies of hadith narrators. He wrote a book called *Al-Dalā'il*, on the differences of opinion between Imam Mālik, Abū Ḥanīfah and Imam al-Shāfiʿī. He died in 392 AH.

81 *Āl ʿImrān*, 61.

82 Reported by Bukhārī (4380) and Muslim (2420) from the hadith of Ḥudhayfah.

83 His full name at the time was ʿAbd al-Masīḥ (meaning "slave of the Messiah") and he was from Kindah, but he later returned to the Prophet ﷺ and accepted Islam.

84 *al-Baqarah*, 23.

to the hearts and tremors in the ears of those who listen to it, and the awe which seizes them due to its high status and the power of its recitation. The effect of the Qur'an is even greater on those who reject it, until they become overwhelmed by what they are hearing. It increases their feelings of alienation and aversion, just as Allah Exalted says in the Qur'an, and the hatred in their hearts makes them wish that the sound would stop.

That is why the Prophet ﷺ said: "Undoubtedly, the Qur'an is hard on the one who dislikes it, and it is the Adjudicator [between truth and falsehood]."[85]

The believers also feel a sense of fear and awe when they hear the Qur'an, but they lean towards it and have their chests expanded. Their mood is brightened by their hearts' inclination towards its recitation, and their firm belief in what it contains. As Allah Exalted mentions: "It is Allah Who has sent down the best message – a Book of perfect consistency and repeated lessons – which causes the skin and hearts of those who fear their Lord to tremble, then their skin and hearts soften at the mention of the Mercy of Allah."[86]

Allah also confirms: "Had We sent this Qur'an upon a mountain, you would have certainly seen it humbled and torn apart in awe of Allah. We set forth such comparisons for people so perhaps they may reflect."[87] This verse illuminates a feature of the Qur'an that is so unique to it that even the one who does not understand its meaning can be affected by it. This is illustrated in the story of the Christian man who came across a person reciting Qur'an, so he came to a halt and began to sob. He was asked why he was crying, and replied: "Because it has broken my heart, and because of the beauty of its arrangement." This same emotion has gripped many

---

85 Reported by Daylamī, and others, from al-Ḥakam ibn ʿUmayr.

86 *al-Zumar*, 23.

87 *al-Ḥashr*, 21.

people before they accepted Islam, and many after; some submitted and believed in the Qur'an from the moment they heard it, whilst others refused.

It is reported in an authentic hadith that Jubayr ibn Muṭʿim said: "I heard the Prophet ﷺ reading Surah al-Ṭūr in the evening (*maghrib*) prayer. When he reached the following verses: "Were they created by nothing, or are they their own creators? Or did they create the heavens and the earth? In fact, they have no firm belief in Allah. Or do they possess the treasuries of your Lord, or are they in control of everything?"[88] I felt like my heart would fly into the sky."[89] And in another chain of narration: "That was the first time that faith (īmān) was instilled in my heart."[90]

It was related from ʿUtbah ibn Rabīʿah that when he spoke to the Prophet ﷺ in regard to his people differing about the revelation of Allah Exalted, the Prophet ﷺ recited to him: "Ḥā Mīm. This is a revelation from the Most Compassionate, Most Merciful. It is a Book whose verses are perfectly explained – a Qur'an in Arabic for people who know, delivering good news and warning. Yet most of them turn away, so they do not hear. They say, 'Our hearts are veiled against what you are calling us to, there is deafness in our ears, and there is a barrier between us and you. So do whatever you want and so shall we!' Say, O Prophet, 'I am only a man like you, but it has been revealed to me that your God is only One God. So take the Straight Way towards Him, and seek His Forgiveness.' And woe to the polytheists – those who do not pay zakat and are in denial of the Hereafter. But those who believe and do good will certainly have a never-ending reward. Ask them, O Prophet, 'How can you disbelieve in the One Who created the earth in two Days? And how can you set up

---

88 *al-Ṭūr*, 35-37.

89 Reported by Bukhārī (4854), and Muslim (463) in an abbreviated narration.

90 Reported by Bukhārī (4023).

equals with Him? That is the Lord of all worlds.' He placed on the earth firm mountains, standing high, showered His blessings upon it, and ordained all its means of sustenance – totaling four Days exactly – for those who ask. Then He turned towards the heaven when it was still like smoke, saying to it and to the earth, 'Submit, willingly or unwillingly.' They both responded, 'We submit willingly.' So He formed the heaven into seven heavens in two Days, assigning to each its mandate. And We adorned the lowest heaven with stars like lamps for beauty and for protection. That is the design of the Almighty, All-Knowing. If they turn away, then say, O Prophet, 'I warn you of a mighty blast, like the one that befell ʿĀd and Thamūd.'"[91] [He ﷺ recited] until ʿUtbah placed his hand on the mouth of the Prophet ﷺ and pleaded with him to stop.[92]

In another chain of narration: the Prophet ﷺ continued to recite until he reached the verse of prostration, whilst ʿUtbah was listening attentively and reclining with his hands behind him. When the Prophet ﷺ performed the prostration, ʿUtbah rose to his feet, not knowing how to respond. He returned to his family and did not go out until the people came to him. He began to apologize, saying: "I swear by Allah, he spoke some words to me that, I swear by Allah, I have never heard anything like. I did not know what to say to him."[93]

Several people have given accounts of attempting to challenge the Prophet ﷺ concerning the Qur'an, but being enveloped in a fear and alarm that stopped them in their tracks. ʿAbdullāh ibn al-Muqaffaʿ[94] had

---

91 *Fuṣṣilat*, 1-13.

92 Reported by Baghawī with this wording, from Jābir ibn ʿAbdullāh, in *Al-Manāhil*, p. 531. Similar hadiths were recorded by Abū Yaʿlā (1818), and others. It was graded as authentic by Ḥākim (2/253), and Dhahabī concurred.

93 Mentioned by Ibn Kathīr in *Al-Sīrah* (1/503-504), in a hadith narrated by Bayhaqī from his teacher Ḥākim, with a chain of transmission back to Muhammad ibn Kaʿb al-Quraẓī.

94 He was originally a Magian but became a Muslim. He was later accused of heresy and killed by the leader of Basra in 132 AH.

precisely that intention and set out on a mission to do so, when he came across a young boy reciting: "And it was said, 'O earth! Swallow up your water'".[95] Immediately, he returned home and erased all his plans, saying: "I bear witness that this speech cannot be replicated; it is not the speech of a man." Furthermore, Ibn al-Muqaffaʿ was one of the most eloquent people of his time.

Yaḥyā ibn Ḥakam al-Ghazzāl[96] was the master of rhetoric in the Andalusia of his day. He relates that he also had a desire to oppose the Qur'an. So, he studied Surah al-Ikhlāṣ with the intention of producing something like it, and began to weave words which, according to his estimation, were following its pattern. He said: "I was held back by fear and numbness, and they carried me towards repentance instead."

The Enduring Nature of the Qur'an

A sure sign of the miraculous status of the Qur'an is that it will remain as an enduring sign for as long as this world exists, because Allah Exalted has promised to protect it. As He states: "It is certainly We Who have revealed the Reminder, and it is certainly We Who will preserve it."[97] "It cannot be proven false from any angle. It is a revelation from the One Who is All-Wise, Praiseworthy."[98]

Most of the miracles that Prophets came with expired after their death, leaving nothing but the memories and reports of those who witnessed them. But the Mighty Qur'an, with its sublime signs and manifest miracles, has prevailed for 535 years from its first revelation until today.[99] The

---

95 *Hūd*, 44.

96 He was Yaḥyā ibn Ḥakam al-Bakrī al-Jayyānī; he was born in 156 AH and died in 250 AH.

97 *al-Ḥijr*, 9.

98 *Fuṣṣilat*, 42.

99 According to the year this text was first written.

Qur’an is a compelling evidence, and any attacks against it are held back. Although every generation was replete with authoritative scholars in language and rhetoric, many of whom were disbelieving and hostile towards us, not one of them was able to contradict the Qur’an in the slightest; they could not even compose two words in opposition! They had no effective form of attack, and any foolish person who tried, had their efforts wasted. In the end, they were overcome by their own incapacity, and forced to turn back on their heels.

Other Miraculous Features of the Qur’an

The reader of the Qur’an never tires of it, and the listener never becomes bored. This is from the many miraculous signs observed by the Muslim population as well as their leaders. Consistently reciting the Qur’an increases its sweetness, and repeating its verses increases the reader in love. Other texts, no matter how beautiful or eloquent, become sour over time, whereas the Qur’an remains fresh at every sitting. Our Book is a joy to read in seclusion, and its recitation reassures at times of crisis. No other book can claim such a status. The people of Qur’an have developed their own intonations and cadences, bringing energy and vitality to their recitations.

The Messenger of Allah ﷺ described the Qur’an when he said: “It does not tire with consistent repetition. Its lessons never end and its wonders do not fade. It is a decisive book, not a mere amusement. The scholars are never full [from its knowledge]. Desires are not misguided by it, and tongues are not confused. It is the one that the jinn said, when they heard it: “‘Indeed we have heard a wondrous recitation.’[100]”[101]

---

100 *al-Jinn*, 1-2.

101 Reported by Tirmidhī (2906), Abū Yaʿlā (367), and others. Narrations with a similar meaning are recorded by Ibn al-Athīr in *Jāmiʿ al-Uṣūl* (8/463-464), on the authority of ʿAbdullāh ibn ʿUmar;

Another miraculous feature of the Qur'an is its explication of knowledge which the Arabs had no awareness of. These were things that none of the scholars of previous generations knew about or had written about. The Qur'an covers the implementation of legal principles and the correct method of adducing intellectual arguments. The revelation pushed back against the sects that had deviated from the truth, using robust proofs, powerful evidence, and clear and concise language. The posers and pretenders wished they could bring evidence like it, but they never could.

As Allah Exalted says: "Can the One Who created the heavens and the earth not easily resurrect these deniers?"[102] "Say, O Prophet, 'They will be revived by the One who produced them the first time.'"[103] "Had there been other gods besides Allah in the heavens or the earth, both realms would have surely been corrupted."[104]

The Qur'an also comprises knowledge of the Sīrah, stories of previous generations, warnings, wisdoms, news of the Hereafter, and guidance to develop excellent morals and character. As Allah Exalted affirms: "We have left nothing out of the Record."[105] "We have certainly set forth every kind of lesson for people in this Qur'an."[106] "We have revealed to you the Book as an explanation of all things."[107]

The Prophet ﷺ said: "Undoubtedly, Allah sent down this Qur'an to command and to warn, as a way to be followed, and an example to be understood. It contains your story, and news of what came before you and what will come after you. It is a judgment between you. It is not

---

and Ḥākim (1/555) from the hadith of ʿAbdullāh ibn Masʿūd, which he graded as authentic.

102 *Yā Sīn*, 81.

103 *Yā Sīn*, 79.

104 *al-Anbiyā*, 22.

105 *al-Anʿām*, 38.

106 *al-Rūm*, 58.

107 *al-Naḥl*, 89.

worn out by lengthy repetition, and its wonders never end. The Qur'an is the truth, not mere amusement. Whoever speaks by it tells the truth, and whoever judges by it is just. Whoever argues by it wins, and whoever swears by it is equitable. Whoever works by it is rewarded, and whoever holds on to it is guided to the straight path. Whoever seeks guidance from elsewhere, Allah causes them to be misguided. Whoever judges by other than the Qur'an, Allah destroys them. It is the Wise Remembrance, the Clear Light, the Straight Path, the Strong Rope of Allah, the Beneficial Cure. It preserves the one who holds on to it, and rescues the one who follows it. There is no crookedness in it, so it sets matters straight. It does not deviate, so does not merit blame or disparagement. Its miracles never cease, neither is it exhausted by lengthy repetition."

A similar narration is reported from Ibn Mas'ūd, who also mentioned: "It does not differ or tire with repetition, and it contains news of the first and the last."[108]

A hadith from Ka'b states that Allah Exalted said to Prophet Muhammad ﷺ: "I am sending down to you a new Torah[109] which will open blind eyes, deaf ears, and enclosed hearts. It contains fountains of knowledge, the understanding of wisdom, and the blossoming of the hearts."[110] Ka'b also narrated: "It is upon yourselves [to hold on to] the Qur'an, because it is the understanding of the intellect, and the light of wisdom."

Allah Exalted says: "Indeed, this Qur'an clarifies for the Children of Israel most of what they differ over."[111]

"This is an insight to humanity – a guide and a lesson to the God-fear-

---

108 Reported by Ḥākim (2/289-290).

109 i.e., the Qur'an.

110 Reported by Ibn al-Ḍurays in *Faḍā'il al-Qur'ān*. A similar narration was reported by Ibn Abī Shaybah in *Al-Muṣannaf*, on the authority of Mughīth ibn Sumayy.

111 *al-Naml*, 76.

ing."[112]

The Qur'an conveys a wealth of meaning through concise terms; the books before it, in contrast, were less in meaning, although more verbose. From its miraculous features, the Qur'an is simultaneously a proof and what is proven. That is because its beautiful composition, eloquence, and precise rhetoric are used as evidence of its inimitability. Within this rhetoric are His command and prohibition, and His promise and threat. The one who recites will understand both the proof of the Qur'an and the obligation upon him, even from a single word or individual surah.

The Qur'an was revealed in a literary form previously unheard of. It is not the poetry previously known by the Arabs. But it is also not prose, because texts arranged into verses are easier on the soul, softer on the heart, sweeter on the ear, and simpler to understand. Because of the mesmerizing style of the Qur'an, people were quick to incline towards it.

It is also miraculous that Allah Exalted has made the Qur'an so easy to memorize and retain. As Allah announces: "And We have certainly made the Qur'an easy to remember."[113] Not one of the previous nations memorized their books, even if they spent years trying to do so. As for the Qur'an, young boys memorize it in a short time and with ease.

The coherence of the Qur'an is incomparable; some sections resemble others; each part sits in harmony with the other; and each story, each idea, and each surah flows beautifully into the next. A single surah may contain commands and prohibitions, news and investigation, promises and threats, confirmation of the Prophethood, affirmation of the Oneness of Allah, evocation of desires and fears, and even more benefits that have not been mentioned. All this is achieved in a seamless fashion, without disturbing the flow of the text. When pure Arabic like this is found outside

---

112 *Āl ʿImrān*, 138.

113 *al-Qamar*, 17.

of the Qur'an it is missing the same luster; it is inevitably weaker in style, lesser in beauty, and imperfect in its wording.

So, reflect on the beginning of Surah Ṣād; it informs us about the disbelievers, the schisms between them, and the examples of previous nations used to reproach them. The surah mentions their denial of our Master Muhammad ﷺ and their astonishment at what he came with. It describes the gathering of their leaders – in order to establish an agreement to persist in their disbelief – and the jealousy in their words. It details their abasement and incapacity, and their promised humiliation in this life and the Hereafter. Ṣād depicts the repeated denials of previous nations and the destruction Allah had prepared for them, and warns contemporary disbelievers that they could end up facing the same fate. The surah also expresses the patience of the Prophet ﷺ in the face of their actions, and the consolation he took from everything we have mentioned. It continues onto the stories of Dāwūd and other Prophets. All this is compiled in the most succinct speech and beautiful arrangement.

As has been mentioned by ourselves and many leading scholars in the field, the combination of concise speech and deep meaning found in the Qur'an is a part of its miraculous nature. This can be summarized in the four features we mentioned previously, so rely on them, but the wonders and special characteristics of the Qur'an never truly come to an end.

Success is with Allah.

The Splitting of the Moon and the Holding Back of the Sun

"The Hour has drawn near, and the Moon was split in two. Yet, whenever they see a sign, they turn away, saying, 'Same old magic.'"[114] Allah Exalted informs us of the splitting of the Moon in the past tense, and de-

---

114 *al-Qamar*, 1-2.

scribes how the disbelievers turned away from His signs. Commentators and people of the Sunnah unanimously agree that this miracle took place.

Al-Ḥusayn ibn Muhammad al-Ḥāfiẓ reports in his book: Sirāj ibn ʿAbdullāh narrated, from al-Aṣīlī, from al-Marwaziyy, from al-Farabrī, from Bukhārī, from Musaddad, from Yaḥyā, from Shuʿbah, and Sufyān, from al-Aʿmash, from Ibrāhīm, from Abū Maʿmar, from Ibn Masʿūd who said: "The Moon was split at the time of the Messenger of Allah ﷺ into two parts: one part was above the mountains, and the other part was below them. The Messenger of Allah ﷺ said: 'Witness!'"[115]

The narration of Mujāhid includes: "...and we were with the Prophet ﷺ."[116] Some of the reports from al-Aʿmash add: "[...and we were] in Minā.[117]"[118] In the hadith of al-Aswad, on the authority of Ibn Masʿūd, the wording includes: "Until I saw the mountains between the two halves of the Moon."[119] According to the narration of Masrūq,[120] it happened in Makkah, and he added: "The disbelievers of Quraysh said: 'The son of Abū Kabshah[121] has enchanted you with magic.' Then one of them said: 'If Muhammad has enchanted the Moon in this way, then surely his magic would not have bewitched the whole world. Ask those who arrive from other lands if they saw it.' So people came and they questioned them, and they confirmed that they had seen it take place."

Al-Samarqandī relates a similar narration from al-Ḍaḥḥāk: "Abū Jahl

---

115 Reported with this chain of narration by Bukhārī (4864). Also recorded by Muslim (2800).

116 Narrated by Mujāhid, from Abū Maʿmar, from Ibn Masʿūd, in Bukhārī (4865).

117 Also known as the City of Tents for its appearance during Hajj, located eight kilometres southeast of Makkah.

118 Reported by Bukhārī (3869) and Muslim (44/2800).

119 Reported by Aḥmad (1/413), and Ṭabarī in *Al-Tafsīr* (27/85).

120 Masrūq ibn al-Ajdaʿ narrated from Ibn Masʿūd. Reported by Bukhārī (3869), al-Ṭayālisī (2447), Ṭabarī (27/58), and Abū Nuʿaym in *Al-Dalāʾil* (211).

121 Abū Kabshah was the father of the Prophet ﷺ by relation of breast-feeding (i.e., the husband of the wet-nurse of the Prophet ﷺ), although there are also other opinions as to his identity.

said: 'This is magic. Send people to the remote areas to see if they witnessed it or not.' The people living in the remote areas confirmed that they had seen the Moon splitting. The disbelievers simply said: 'This is continuous magic.'" It was also reported by 'Alqamah, again from 'Abdullāh ibn Mas'ūd. It was also narrated by Anas,[122] Ibn 'Abbās,[123] Ibn 'Umar,[124] Ḥudhayfah,[125] 'Alī,[126] and Jubayr ibn Muṭ'im.[127] 'Alī said, in the narration from Ḥudhayfah al-Arḥabī: "The Moon split whilst we were with the Prophet ﷺ."

Anas said: "The people of Makkah asked the Prophet ﷺ to show them a sign. So he showed them the splitting of the Moon into two parts, until they could see Ḥirā'[128] in between." Qatādah also related this from Anas.

In the narration of Ma'mar, and others, from Qatādah: "He showed the splitting of the Moon and Allah Exalted revealed: 'The Hour has drawn near and the Moon was split in two.'"[129] It was also related from Jubayr ibn Muṭ'im, his son Muhammad, and his grandson Jubayr ibn Muhammad, and it was narrated by 'Ubaydullāh ibn 'Abdullāh ibn 'Utbah, from Ibn 'Abbās. Mujāhid relates it from from Ibn 'Umar, and Ḥudhayfah relates it from 'Abd al-Raḥmān al-Sulamiyy,[130] and Muslim ibn Abī 'Imrān al-Azdī.

---

122 Reported by Bukhārī (3637) and Muslim (2802).

123 Reported by Bukhārī (3638) and Muslim (2803).

124 Reported by Muslim (2801).

125 Found in *Al-Manāhil,* p. 540, where it is transmitted from Ibn Jarīr, Ibn Abī Ḥātim, and Abū Nu'aym.

126 Reported by Bayhaqī in *Al-Dalā'il.*

127 Reported by Tirmidhī (3289). It was graded as authentic by Ḥākim (2/472), and Dhahabī agreed.

128 A mountain to the northeast of Makkah.

129 *al-Qamar,* 1.

130 He is 'Abdullāh ibn Ḥabīb, a great man from the Followers, a trusted narrator, and a firm reciter. A second opinion states that he is Muhammad ibn al-Ḥusayn, a leading scholar in the field of hadith who died in 412 AH.

Most of these hadiths have the most authentic chains of narration, and the Qur'anic verse clarifies [that this miracle took place]. One should not turn their attention to the objections of those who had become disheartened; the ones who suggested that if this miracle had indeed taken place, then it would not have been concealed from anyone in the world. It has not been transmitted to us from other communities that they spotted the splitting of the Moon on that night, although even if it had been transmitted from people who were known liars it would not have been a proof for us. Regardless, the Moon does not have the same appearance for every community in the world at any given time. It could rise for one people before it rises for another. It could take the opposite appearance from one side of the Earth to the other. Or, it could be obscured from a people by clouds or mountains. Similarly, you find eclipses of the Moon that were witnessed in some lands and not in others, and as partial eclipses in some places and full eclipses in others. In some areas, only those who claim to have knowledge recognize these eclipses. "That is the design of the Almighty, the All-Knowing."[131]

The miracle of the Moon took place at night. The custom of people at night is for quietness and tranquility, and to stay at home and lock their doors. People do not notice much happening in the sky at night, except for those who specifically pay attention to it. For example, although there are many eclipses of the Moon, most people do not know about them until they are informed by others. There are many reliable reports of majestic stars and lights rising in the sky at night, yet most of us have never heard of these miraculous events.

Al-Ṭaḥāwī[132] reported from Asmā' bint 'Umays, in an obscure hadith,

---

131 *Yā Sīn*, 38.

132 He is also known as Abū Ja'far, and his full name is Aḥmad ibn Muhammad al-Ṭaḥāwī, an Imam, leading scholar, and great memorizer of texts. He was the foremost authority on hadiths and jurisprudence in Egypt. Al-Ṭaḥāwī was born in 239 AH and died in 321 AH. His works include

that the Prophet ﷺ was resting his head on ʿAlī's lap and began to receive revelation, until the Sun had set and the time for the ʿaṣr (mid-afternoon) prayer had passed. The Messenger of Allah ﷺ said: "ʿAlī! Did I pray?" He replied: "No." Then, the Messenger of Allah ﷺ said: "Allah! If it is in obedience to You, and obedience to Your Messenger, then return the Sun upon me." Asmā' said: "I saw the Sun set, and then I saw it rise after it had set, and it stopped between the mountains and the Earth. This happened at al-Ṣahbā', in Khaybar."[133] Al-Ṭaḥāwī noted that Aḥmad ibn Sāliḥ used to say: "The one seeking knowledge should memorize the hadith of Asmā' because it contains signs of the Prophethood."

Yūnus ibn Bukayr narrated from Ibn Isḥāq: "When the Messenger of Allah ﷺ went on the Night Journey, and informed his people of an approaching caravan and its company as a sign to them, they asked: "When will it arrive?" The Prophet ﷺ replied: "Thursday." When the day arrived, the Quraysh began looking out for it, until the whole day had passed and the caravan still had not arrived. The Prophet ﷺ prayed to Allah: "Increase the day by an hour", and the Sun was held back.[134]

When Water Flowed from between the Fingers of the Prophet ﷺ

There are numerous hadiths about the occasion when water flowed from between the fingers of the Prophet ﷺ, narrated by several of the Companions including Anas, Jābir, and Ibn Masʿūd.

Abū Isḥāq reported: "Ibrāhīm ibn Jaʿfar al-Faqīh and his father both

---

Al-Maṭbū'ah: Sharḥ Ma'ānī al-Āthār; Al-ʿAqīdat al-Ṭaḥāwiyyah; and *Sharḥ Mushkil al-Āthār,* which was published in sixteen volumes by Mu'assasat al-Risālah.

133 This hadith was related with chains of transmission from Asmā' bint ʿUmays, Abū Hurayrah, ʿAlī ibn Abī Ṭālib, and Abū Saʿīd al-Khudrī. Its status was affirmed by Ibn Taymiyyah, and he was followed in his opinion by his student, and scholar in his own right, Ibn Qayyim al-Jawziyyah.

134 Mentioned by Ibn Kathīr in *Shamā'il al-Rasūl,* p. 546.

read to us, from ʿĪsā ibn Sahl, from Abū al-Qāsim (also known as Ḥātim ibn Muhammad), from Abū ʿUmar ibn al-Fakhkhār, from Abū ʿĪsā, from Yaḥyā, from Mālik, from Isḥāq ibn ʿAbdullāh ibn Abī Ṭalḥah, from Anas ibn Mālik : 'I saw the Messenger of Allah ﷺ at the time of the ʿaṣr prayer. The people were looking for water to make *wuḍū'* but they could not find any, so the Messenger of Allah ﷺ brought it. The Messenger of Allah ﷺ made *wuḍū'* and then he placed his hand into the container holding the water. He told the people to make *wuḍū'* from it. I saw the water flowing from between his fingers. All the people made *wuḍū'* from it, down to the last man.'"[135] The same hadith was related from Anas by Qatādah, who mentions: "The water in the container completely or almost completely submerged his fingers." Qatādah was asked: "How many were you?" He replied: "We were around three hundred."[136]

Another version of the narration from Qatādah says: "And they were in the *sūq* (market) in al-Zawrā'[137]."[138] The hadith was also reported from Anas by Ḥumayd, Thābit, and al-Ḥasan. Ḥumayd and Thābit said there were eighty people.[139] Other narrations from Thābit put the figure at seventy,[140] between seventy and eighty,[141] or between sixty and eighty.[142]

Ibn Masʿūd relates in an authentic hadith from the transmission of ʿAlqamah: "We were with the Messenger of Allah ﷺ and had no water, so he said to us: 'Ask who has some water.' Water was brought, and he poured

135 Reported by Bukhārī (169), and with this chain of translation by Muslim (2279/5).

136 Reported by Bukhārī (3572) and Muslim (2279/7).

137 A place in Madinah, to the west of the Mosque of the Prophet ﷺ. There was a market there during the early days of Islam, as recorded by our teacher Muhammad Shurrāb, on p. 135 of *Al-Muʿālim al-Athīrah*.

138 Reported by Bukhārī (3572) and Muslim (2279/6).

139 The hadith from Ḥumayd was reported by Bukhārī (3575).

140 This was the transmission of al-Ḥasan al-Baṣrī, from Anas. Reported by Bukhārī (3574).

141 Reported by Bukhārī (200).

142 Reported by Muslim (2279/4).

it into a container and placed his hand in it. The water started to spring from between the fingers of the Messenger of Allah ﷺ."[143]

Sālim ibn Abī al-Jaʿd narrates an authentic hadith from Jābir : "The people were thirsty on the day of al-Ḥudaybiyyah, and Messenger of Allah ﷺ had a water vessel in front of him. He made *wuḍū'* from it, and indicated for the people to do the same. We had no water except what was in that vessel. As the Prophet ﷺ placed his hand into the water vessel, the water began to cascade from between his fingers like flowing springs." When Jābir was asked how many people they were, he replied: "If we had been one hundred thousand, the water would have sufficed, but we were fifteen hundred." Anas narrated something similar from Jābir,[144] and concurred that they were at al-Ḥudaybiyyah.

ʿUbādah ibn al-Walīd ibn ʿUbādah ibn al-Ṣāmit narrates, also from Jābir, in a long hadith about the Patrol of Buwāṭ: "The Messenger of Allah ﷺ said to me: 'Jābir! Call for water to make *wuḍū'*.' Nothing was found except a drop in a dried animal skin. It was brought to the Prophet ﷺ and he squeezed it, saying something I could not make out. He told me to bring a bowl. I brought it, and he placed it between his hands." The Prophet ﷺ then stretched his hand into the bowl and spread his fingers, and Jābir said: "In the name of Allah" and poured the water. "I saw the water cascading from between his fingers. The water gushed and flowed until the bowl was full, and he told the people to use it until everyone had fulfilled their need. The Messenger of Allah ﷺ lifted his hand from the bowl and it was still full."[145]

Al-Shaʿbī[146] reported: "On one of his journeys, the Prophet ﷺ was

---

143 Reported by Bukhārī (3579), and Dārimī (29). Also refer to the *Musnad* of Abū Yaʿlā (5372).

144 Reported by Dārimī (28).

145 Reported by Muslim (3013).

146 He is ʿĀmir ibn Sharāḥīl al-Shaʿbī: a reliable narrator from the Followers and an expert in jurisprudence, and he died at around eighty years of age.

brought a water container and was told: 'Messenger of Allah! This is all the water we have.' He poured it into a bowl, and dipped his finger into the centre. All the people came, made *wuḍū'*, and left again."[147]

The story was also recorded by Tirmidhī from ʿImrān ibn Ḥuṣayn.

These events happened in places where many people gathered, so the above reports do not merit any doubt or debate. The Companions who narrated them were the quickest to challenge falsehood whenever they heard it, and they would never remain silent in the face of a lie. They narrated these hadiths, circulated them to a great number of a people, and attributed them to the Prophet ﷺ. No-one objected to the hadiths attributed to them, and their agreement serves as a collective confirmation of the events that took place.

The Flowing of Water by the Blessing (*Barakah*) of the Prophet ﷺ

In a hadith on the Expedition to Tabūk, Muʿādh narrates that they had reached a spring which was spurting water in bursts. They scooped the water with their hands until they had gathered a small amount. The Prophet ﷺ washed his face and hands, and allowed the water to drip back into the bowl. Suddenly, the bowl was overflowing with water, and everyone drank from it. Ibn Isḥāq commented: "The water erupted as quickly as lightning." [148] Then the Prophet ﷺ said: "Muʿādh! If you have a long life, you will see what is here fill gardens."[149]

In the hadith of al-Barā' ibn ʿĀzib[150] and Salamah ibn al-Akwaʿ[151]

---

147 A *mursal* hadith.

148 The hadith of Ibn Isḥāq is mentioned by Ibn Hishām in *Al-Sīrah* (2/527) without the chain of transmission.

149 The hadith of Muʿādh is reported by Mālik in *Al-Muwaṭṭa'* (1/143-144), and by Muslim in *Al-Faḍā'il* (706/10) with the chain of Mālik.

150 Reported by Bukhārī (3577).

151 Reported by Muslim (1729).

(who gave a fuller account) regarding the story of al-Ḥudaybiyyah, they were fourteen hundred people, and the well was not enough to quench fifty sheep. The narration continues: "We crowded around and did not leave a single drop. The Prophet ﷺ sat at the mouth of the well." Al-Barā' added: "The Prophet ﷺ was brought a bucket from the well and he spat in it and supplicated." Salamah said: "Either he supplicated or he spat into it, and the water burst out. We had enough for ourselves and our containers." Ibn Shihāb said, in a separate chain of transmission: "The Prophet ﷺ took out an arrow from its holder and stuck it into the bottom of a dry well. Water flowed freely until that particular well became a favourite spot for quenching their animals' thirst."

Abū Qatādah mentions that people complained to the Messenger of Allah ﷺ of thirst during one of their travels. He called for a type of vessel used to make *wuḍū'*, held it under his arm, and covered its mouth. Allah knows best if he blew into it or not. The people drank from the vessel until they were satisfied, and every one of the seventy-two men present had their containers filled. A similar hadith was narrated from 'Imrān ibn Ḥuṣayn.

Ṭabarī records a different version of the hadith from Abū Qatādah, saying that the Prophet ﷺ went to the people of Mu'tah when he had heard of the killing of their leaders. In a long hadith, he relates several miracles and signs of the Prophet ﷺ, including the story of the water vessel on the day they were without water. He says they were roughly three hundred people. The Prophet ﷺ said to Abū Qatādah:[152] "Look after this water vessel of yours, because it is going to be significant."

'Imrān ibn Ḥuṣayn also speaks about the Prophet ﷺ and his companions being afflicted by thirst on a journey. He turned to two men from the group and said that they would find a woman at a certain place, and that she would have a camel carrying two water-skins. They found her,

---

152 This sentence is from the wording of the hadith recorded by Muslim (681).

and took her to the Prophet ﷺ. He poured from the water-skins into a container and recited over it whatever Allah wished. He then returned the water into the two skins. He opened them up and called the people, until every last one had filled their container. ʿImrān said: "It seemed as if the water-skins were even fuller than before." The Prophet ﷺ then ordered the people to gather provisions for the woman, until she had filled her garment. Then he said to her: "Go, for we have not taken a single drop of your water. Rather, Allah has quenched our thirst."

It is related from Salamah ibn al-Akwaʿ: "The Prophet ﷺ said: 'Is there any water for *wuḍū'*?' A man came with a vessel containing a few drops and emptied it into a bowl. The water was splashing at every one of us, and we – fourteen hundred people – made *wuḍū'* from that bowl."[153]

ʿUmar describes their state in the hadith concerning the army of ʿUsrah. So severe was their thirst, a man was ready to kill his camel, squeeze its stomach and drink the contents. Abū Bakr asked the Prophet ﷺ to supplicate, so he raised his hands, and he did not bring them back down until they sky had spilled over (i.e., the rain began to pour), and they filled all the containers they had. The rain did not extend beyond where the army was stationed.[154]

ʿAmr ibn Shuʿayb narrates an occasion when Abū Ṭālib was riding with the Prophet ﷺ at Dhū al-Majāz[155]. Abū Ṭālib said to the Prophet ﷺ: "I am thirsty but I do not have any water." The Prophet ﷺ got down and struck the ground with his foot, and water burst out. He said: "Drink."[156]

There are many more hadiths on this topic, including those describing the Prophet ﷺ praying and supplicating for rain.

---

153 Reported by Muslim (1729).

154 Reported by Bazzār in *Kashf al-Astār* (1841).

155 The name of a particular marketplace.

156 Suyūṭī attributes the hadith to Ibn Saʿd, in *Al-Manāhil*, p. 555.

The Prophet ﷺ Miraculously Increasing Food through His Blessings and Supplications

The esteemed Abū ʿAlī informed us of a hadith related to him from al-ʿUdhrī, from al-Rāzī, from al-Julūdī, from Ibn Sufyān, from Muslim ibn al-Ḥajjāj, from Salamah ibn Shabīb, from al-Ḥasan ibn Aʿyan, from Maʿqil, from Abū al-Zubayr, from Jābir, who said: "A man came to the Prophet ﷺ asking for food, so he gave him half a *wasq*[157] of barley. The man, his wife, and his guests continued to eat from the barley, until eventually he weighed it again. The Prophet ﷺ came and said: 'If you had not weighed it, you would have continued to eat from it, and it would have remained with you.'"[158]

There is also the famous hadith of Abū Ṭalḥah, where the Prophet ﷺ fed seventy or eighty men from a few loaves of barley bread that Anas had brought under his arm. The Prophet ﷺ asked for them to be broken into pieces and recited over them whatever Allah wished.[159]

Jābir mentions an occasion at the Battle of the Trench, when the Prophet ﷺ fed one thousand people from a *ṣāʿ*[160] of barley and a lamb. Jābir said: "I swear by Allah, after everyone had eaten, the food remained as before. Our dough was being baked into bread, and the Prophet ﷺ would spit into it with blessings." Saʿīd ibn Mīnā' and Ayman also narrated the hadith from Jābir.[161]

Thābit relates a similar hadith from a man from the Anṣār and his wife – they were not named. He said: "He came with about a handful [of barley] and the Prophet ﷺ scattered it into the pot, reciting over it whatever

157 A measurement of weight.

158 Reported by Muslim (2281).

159 Reported by Bukhārī (3578), and Muslim (2040).

160 Another measurement of weight.

161 The narration of Saʿīd ibn Mīnā' is reported by Bukhārī (4102), and Muslim (2039). The hadith of Ayman, narrated by his son ʿAbd al-Wāḥid, is reported by Bukhārī (4101).

Allah wished. Everyone in the house ate from it until they were full, and afterwards the same amount remained in the pot."[162]

Abū Ayyūb narrates that he had prepared just enough food for the Prophet ﷺ and Abū Bakr. The Prophet ﷺ said to him: "Call for thirty of the nobles of the Anṣār." So he called for them, and they ate until they left. The Prophet ﷺ said: "Call for sixty [of them]." The same thing happened. Then he said: "Call for seventy [of them]." The same thing happened again, and not one person left without becoming a Muslim and pledging their allegiance to the Prophet ﷺ. Abū Ayyūb commented: "So altogether, 180 people ate from my food."[163] Samurah ibn Jundub reports that the Prophet ﷺ was once brought a plate of meat, and people came to eat all the way from morning till night. One group would stand up to leave, and another would enter and sit.[164]

ʿAbd al-Raḥmān ibn Abī Bakr relates: "There were 130 of us with the Prophet ﷺ." The hadith mentions that a *ṣāʿ* of flour was kneaded, a sheep was prepared, and its offal was roasted. ʿAbd al-Raḥmān said: "I swear by Allah, there was not one of the 130 who did not get a slice of the offal. The meat was then served on two plates, and we all ate from both." Some food was still left, and he loaded it onto a camel.

Hadiths narrated by ʿAbd al-Raḥmān ibn Abī ʿAmrah al-Anṣārī from his father,[165] Salamah ibn al-Akwaʿ,[166] Abū Hurayrah,[167] and ʿUmar ibn

---

162 Suyūṭī attributes the hadith to Ibn Saʿd, in *Al-Manāhil,* p. 559.

163 Reported by Haythamī in *Majmaʿ al-Zawāʾid* (8/303).

164 Reported by Tirmidhī (3625), and others. Graded as authentic by Ibn Ḥibbān in *Mawārid* (2149), Ḥākim (2/618), and Dhahabī concurred with him, and Bayhaqī.

165 Reported by Aḥmad (3/417,418), Nasāʾī in ʿAmal al-*Yawm wa al-Laylah* (1140), Ṭabarānī (575), and graded as authentic by Ibn Ḥibbān in *Al-Iḥsān* (221). Also authenticated by Ḥākim (2/618-619), and Dhahabī concurred. Haythamī said in *Majmaʿ al-Zawāʾid* (28): "Its narrators are reliable."

166 Reported by Bukhārī (2484), and Muslim (1729).

167 Reported by Muslim (27).

al-Khaṭṭāb,[168] mention the extreme hunger that afflicted the people during one of the raids with the Prophet ﷺ. He called for the remaining provisions, and each person brought a handful of food or more. The most anyone brought was a *ṣāʿ* of dates. The Prophet ﷺ gathered it all on a mat. Salamah said: "I estimated it to amount to the equivalent of a goat." Then he called for the people; every single container was filled with food, and there was still more remaining.

Abū Hurayrah said: "The Prophet ﷺ told me to call for the People of al-Ṣuffah[169]. I went around until I had gathered them, and a dish of food was placed in front of them. We ate as much as we liked. When we left, the dish was just as when it had arrived, except for our fingermarks."[170]

ʿAlī ibn Abī Ṭālib said: "The Messenger of Allah ﷺ gathered together forty people from the tribe of Banū ʿAbd al-Muṭṭalib. Some of them were eating a lamb and drinking from a large, twelve-*mudd*[171] vessel. He prepared them a *mudd* of food and they ate until they were satiated. The amount of food remained as it was before. Then he called for a large mug, and they drank until they had quenched their thirst. Again, the amount remained as if untouched."[172]

Anas reports: "When the Prophet ﷺ had a house built for Zaynab, he told me to call for certain people he mentioned by name, as well as anyone I came across. The people came until the house was completely full. A pot was brought out containing about one *mudd* of *ḥays*[173]. It was placed in

---

168 Reported by Abū Yaʿlā (230), and Suyūṭī in *Al-Manāhil,* p. 563. Also mentioned by Haythamī in *Majmaʿ al-Zawāʾid* (8/304).

169 Poor people who used to live in the Mosque of the Prophet ﷺ.

170 Mentioned by Haythamī in *Majmaʿ al-Zawāʾid* (8/308).

171 A *mudd* is a measurement of weight equal to 1.032 litres or 815.39 grams.

172 Reported by Aḥmad (1/159), Suyūṭī in *Al-Manāhil,* p. 564, and others. Also mentioned by Haythamī in *Majmaʿ al-Zawāʾid* (8/308).

173 A dish made from crushed dates and preserved butter, mixed with camels' milk cheese or flour.

front of the Prophet ﷺ, and he dipped three of his fingers into the dish. People were eating and then getting up to leave, but the amount of food remained as before. There were seventy-one or seventy-two people that day."[174] In another wording of the story, there were about three hundred people, and they all ate until satiated.[175] Anas adds that the Prophet ﷺ told him to take the plate away, and he could not tell if it contained more or less food than when he first set it down.

Ja'far ibn Muhammad narrates from his father, from 'Alī that Fāṭimah cooked a pot of food for lunch, and she sent 'Alī to the Prophet ﷺ so that he could come to eat with them. The Prophet ﷺ told her to prepare a serving for each of his wives, then for himself, then for 'Alī, and then for herself. After that, Fāṭimah opened the pot and it was overflowing. She said: "Whatever we ate was as Allah wished."[176]

On another occasion, the Prophet ﷺ ordered 'Umar ibn al-Khaṭṭāb to prepare provisions for four hundred riders from the Aḥmas tribe. 'Umar said: "Messenger of Allah! There is nothing except a few *ṣā'*." The Prophet ﷺ repeated: "Go." So he went, and provided them from what they had: a pot of dates, equivalent in weight to a small, kneeling camel. After they had eaten, the pot was still as full as before. The same hadith is related by Dukayn al-Aḥmasī[177] and Jarīr. Al-Nu'mān ibn Muqarrin relates an almost identical hadith, except that he said they were "four hundred riders from Muzīnah."[178]

Jabīr mentions a debt his father left after passing away. Jābir offered

---

174 Reported by Muslim (1428/95), and partially recorded by Bukhārī (5170).

175 Reported by Muslim (1428/95) from the hadith of Anas ibn Mālik.

176 Suyūṭī said in *Al-Manāhil*, p. 566: "The chain of transmission of Ibn Sa'd is disconnected."

177 Reported by Aḥmad (4/174), Ṭabarānī (4210), and others. Graded as authentic by Abū Nu'aym in *Al-Ḥilyah* (1/365), and Ibn Ḥibbān in *Mawārid* (2151). Also mentioned by Haythamī in *Majma' al-Zawā'id* (8/304-305).

178 Reported by Aḥmad (5/445). Its chain of transmission was declared as authentic by Haythamī in *Majma' al-Zawā'id* (8/304), and Suyūṭī in *Al-Manāhil*, p. 567.

the creditors some land containing date palm trees, but they would not accept, and it was clear that years of harvesting the fruits from the trees would not have sufficed to settle the debt. The Prophet ﷺ told him to pick the fruits anyway, and then came to him. After paying the creditors what they were owed, in full, Jābir was left with a full year's harvest of the dates.[179] In another wording of the hadith, he was left with the same amount as he had paid.[180] Jābir said: "The creditors, who were Jews, were amazed by that."

Abū Huraryah narrated: "The people were afflicted by severe hunger. The Messenger of Allah ﷺ said to me: 'Is there anything [to eat]?' I answered: 'Yes, the provisions contain some dates.' The Prophet ﷺ said: 'Bring them to me.' He took out a handful of the dates, opened his palm and supplicated. Then he said: 'Call for ten people.' They ate until they were full, and then another ten did the same. Until the whole army had eaten and filled their stomachs. The Prophet ﷺ said to me: 'Take what you came with and put your hand inside, and hold the bag firmly and do not tip it upside down.' I took out a handful, and found myself with more than I had arrived with in the first place, so I ate from it. I continued to eat from the same dates for the rest of the life of the Messenger of Allah ﷺ, the life of Abū Bakr, the life of ʿUmar, right up until ʿUthmān was killed. After that, it was looted from me."[181] In another version of the hadith, Abū Hurayrah recalls: "I used to carry such-and-such an amount of dates in the cause of Allah."[182] Similar was mentioned in the story of the Expedition to Tabūk, when he had about ten dates.[183]

---

179 Reported by Bukhārī (2127).

180 Reported by Bukhārī (3580).

181 Mentioned by Ibn Kathīr in *Shamā'il al-Rasūl*, pp. 222-223.

182 Reported by Tirmidhī (3839), and Aḥmad (2/352).

183 Reported by Muslim (27/45) on the authority of al-Aʿmash, who was not sure if he had heard the hadith from Abū Ṣāliḥ, or Abū Hurayrah, or Abū Saʿīd.

Abū Huraryah also mentions a time that he was struck by hunger. The Prophet ﷺ asked him to follow. He found a cup of milk that had been given to him as a present, and he told Abū Huraryah to call for the People of al-Ṣuffah. Abū Hurayrah recalls: "I thought: 'What! Is this milk for them? Surely I have more right to drink it in order to regain my strength.' I called for the People of al-Ṣuffah and remembered that the Prophet ﷺ had told me to let them drink. So, I gave one of them to drink, until he was satisfied, then the next person and the next, until they had all had quenched their thirst. The Prophet ﷺ took the cup and said: 'You and I remain. Sit and drink.' So I drank, and then the Prophet ﷺ repeated: 'Drink.' He kept telling me to drink more, until eventually I said: 'No! I swear by the One who sent you with the truth, I cannot find any space for it!' The Prophet ﷺ took the cup, praised Allah, said '*bismillāh*', and drank what was left."[184]

Khālid ibn ʿAbd al-ʿUzzā said that he once prepared a sheep for the Prophet ﷺ. Khālid had a large family, so usually when he slaughtered a sheep it would not be enough for all his children to have a portion. The Prophet ﷺ ate from the sheep he had prepared, put what was left back into the pot, and supplicated for blessings on the food. The meat was distributed to the entire family, and there was still some left over.[185]

Al-Ājurrī narrates a hadith about the Prophet ﷺ marrying his daughter Fāṭimah to ʿAlī. The Prophet ﷺ told Bilāl to bring a pot that could hold four or five *mudd*s and to slaughter a camel for the wedding feast (*walīmah*). He brought the camel, and it was slaughtered. The people came in, one group after another, and everyone ate their fill. The Prophet ﷺ blessed the food that was left over, and instructed for it to be taken to

---

184 Reported by Bukhārī (6452).

185 Mentioned by al-Dūlābī in *Al-Kunā wa al-Asmā'* (1/68). Also reported by Nasāʾī in *Al-Kunā*, al-Ḥasan ibn Sufyān in his *Musnad*, Bayhaqī in *Al-Dalā'il*, and others. It was recorded with an alternative chain of transmission by Ṭabarānī in *Al-Kabīr*, and Haythamī in *Majmaʿ al-Zawā'id* (3/280).

his wives. He said to them: "Eat and enjoy your meal."[186]

Anas relates a story of the Prophet ﷺ getting married: "My mother, Umm Sulaym, prepared some *ḥays*. She gave me the pot to take to the Prophet ﷺ. He said to me: 'Leave it here, and go and invite So-and-so for me, and whoever you meet.' I went and invited them, as well as every single person I met." Anas mentions that they came to roughly three hundred people, filling the house and the back of the mosque. Anas continues: "The Prophet ﷺ said to them, 'Sit in groups of ten.' Then he placed his hand over the food and began to supplicate. The people ate until everyone was full. The Prophet ﷺ told me to take the food away, and I could not tell if it was more or less than when I had first put it down."[187]

The majority of the hadiths in this section are of the highest grade of authenticity. Ten of the Companions agreed on their meaning, and many of the Followers and those who came later narrated from them. Most of these hadiths are found in well-known collections. It is impossible to characterize them as anything but the truth, or to think that anyone present would have been silent about any discrepancies.

The Tree that Answered the Call of the Prophet ﷺ

Aḥmad ibn Muhammad ibn Ghalbūn, the righteous scholar, reports from Abū ʿUmar al-Ṭalamankī, from Abū Bakr ibn al-Muhandis, from Abū al-Qāsim al-Baghawī, from Aḥmad ibn ʿImrān al-Akhnasī, from Abū Ḥayyān al-Taymī, from Mujāhid, from Ibn ʿUmar, who said: "We were with the Messenger of Allah ﷺ on a journey, when he was approached by a Bedouin man. He asked the man where he was going, and he replied: 'To my family'. The Prophet ﷺ said: 'Shall I direct you to something beneficial?' The man replied: 'What is it?' He said: 'For you to bear witness that

186 Mentioned by Suyūṭī in *Al-Manāhil*, p. 572 without naming the narrator.

187 Reported by Bukhārī (5163) and Muslim (1428/94).

there is no deity worthy of worship except Allah, alone and without partners, and that Muhammad is His slave and Messenger.' The man asked: 'Who will testify to what you say?' The Prophet ﷺ answered: 'This acacia tree at the edge of the wadi.' The tree advanced until it stood in front of the Prophet ﷺ and testified three times to what he had said. Then, it returned to its place."[188]

Buraydah narrates: "A Bedouin man asked the Prophet ﷺ for a sign. So he told him: 'Say to that tree: "The Messenger of Allah ﷺ is calling you."' The tree leaned to the right and to the left, then forwards and backwards, before pulling up its roots from the ground. It came, dragging its dusty roots, until it stood in front of the Messenger of Allah ﷺ and greeted him. The Bedouin said: 'Command the tree to return to its original place.' So it did return, replanted its roots, and came to rest. The man said to the Prophet ﷺ: 'Allow me to prostrate to you.' The Prophet ﷺ replied: 'If I were to have ordered any person to prostrate to another, it would have been a woman to her husband.' He said: 'Allow me to kiss your hands and your feet', and he did."[189]

Jābir ibn ʿAbdullāh relates a lengthy hadith, in which the Messenger of Allah ﷺ went to relieve himself but could not find anything to shield himself with. He went to two trees at the edge of the wadi, and held a branch of one of them, saying: "Let me lead you by the permission of Allah." The Prophet ﷺ led the tree, like a camel being led on a halter. He did the same with the other tree until they were level, and said: "Link together in front of me, by the permission of Allah." In another version of the hadith, he said: "Jābir! Tell this tree that the Prophet ﷺ says: 'Join

---

188 Reported by Bazzār (2411), Dārimī (16), Abū Yaʿlā (5662), Ṭabarānī (13582), and others. It was graded as authentic by Ibn Ḥibbān in *Mawārid* (2110), Būṣīrī, and Suyūṭī in *Al-Manāhil*, p. 574. Ibn Kathīr mentions the hadith in *Shamā'il al-Rasūl*, p. 238, and Haythamī says in *Majmaʿ al-Zawā'id* (8/292): "It is related by Ṭabarānī with reliable narrators."

189 Reported by Bazzār (3/132). Haythamī says in *Majmaʿ al-Zawā'id* (8/292): "The chain of transmission of Bazzār contains Ṣāliḥ ibn Ḥibbān, and he was a weak narrator.

with your companion so I can sit behind you both.'" The tree did as it was asked, and the Prophet ﷺ sat behind them. Jābir continues: "I went away and sat down, talking to myself. When I turned, the Prophet ﷺ was coming and the two trees had separated, each standing upright on its trunk. The Prophet ﷺ paused and was gesturing with his head to the right and to the left."[190]

Usāmah ibn Zayd tells a similar story: "During one of the raids, the Messenger of Allah ﷺ asked me: 'Is there anywhere?' Meaning, a place to relieve himself. I said: 'There is no such place in the wadi.' He said: 'Can you see a palm tree or a stone?' I replied that I could see some palm trees. He said: 'Go to them and say: "The Messenger of Allah ﷺ orders you to come to his aid", and say the same thing to the stones.' I swear by the One that sent him with the truth that, when I did so, I saw the palm trees leaning together until they joined, and the stones gathering into a pile. When the Prophet ﷺ had finished, he said to me: 'Tell them to part.' I swear by the One with my soul in His hand, I saw the palm trees and the stones separating until they all returned to their original places."

Yaʿlā ibn Murrah said: "I was travelling with the Prophet ﷺ..." and mentions something similar to the two previous hadiths. "He ordered two small palm trees, so they joined together."[191] In another wording of the hadith: "two things". Ghaylān ibn Salamah mentioned "two trees".[192] Ibn Masʿūd said it was during the Battle of Ḥunayn.

Yaʿlā also mentions some other things he saw from the Prophet ﷺ. He remembers a date palm (or acacia tree) coming over, circling them, and then returning to its original place. The Prophet ﷺ said: "It asked for

---

190 Reported by Muslim (3012). See also, *Majmaʿ al-Zawāʾid* (9/7).

191 Reported by Aḥmad (4/172). Haythamī says in *Majmaʿ al-Zawāʾid* (9/6-7): "It is related by Aḥmad and Ṭabarānī with a good chain of transmission."

192 Ibn Kathīr attributes this wording of the hadith to Ibn ʿAsākir in *Shamāʾil al-Rasūl*, p. 270.

permission to greet me."[193]

Ibn Mas'ūd relates: "A tree announced the presence of the jinn to the Prophet ﷺ, on a night they were listening to him."[194] Mujāhid narrates from Ibn Mas'ūd, in the same hadith, that the jinn said: "Who will testify for you?" The Prophet ﷺ replied: "This tree. Come, tree!" It came, rumbling and dragging its roots.

This story was agreed upon by Ibn 'Umar, Buraydah, Jābir, Ibn Mas'ūd, Ya'lā ibn Murrah, Usāmah ibn Zayd, Anas ibn Mālik, 'Alī ibn Abī Ṭālib, Ibn 'Abbās, and others. It was narrated from them by many of the Followers, and is strengthened by such a number of witnesses.

Ibn Fūrak notes: "Once, the Prophet ﷺ was travelling at night, during the Siege of Ṭā'if, and he was feeling drowsy. His path was intercepted by a lote tree; suddenly, the tree split into two halves, allowing the Prophet ﷺ to pass through." Both trunks remain standing to this day and they are well-known.

Anas tells of an occasion when Jibrīl saw that the Prophet ﷺ was sad, so he said to him: "Would you like me to show you a sign?" The Prophet ﷺ replied that he would. So Jibrīl pointed him to a tree beyond the wadi and said: "Call that tree." The tree came across, until it stood in front of the Prophet ﷺ. Then Jibrīl said: "Order it to return to its place", and it did so.[195] 'Alī gives a similar account, except that he does not mention Jibrīl. In it, the Prophet ﷺ said: "Allah! Show me a such a sign that I will never feel troubled by the ones who deny me again." His sadness was on account of the denials of his people and he was requesting a sign for their sake, rather than for himself.

---

193 Reported by Aḥmad (4/173). Haythamī says in *Majma' al-Zawā'id* (9/6): "It is related by Aḥmad and Ṭabarānī with two chains of transmission, one of which consists of reliable narrators."

194 Reported by Bukhārī (3859) and Muslim (450).

195 Reported by Aḥmad (3/113), Ibn Mājah (4028), Abū Ya'lā (3685, 3686), and Dārimī. Also mentioned by Ibn Kathīr in *Shamā'il al-Rasūl,* p. 235.

Ibn Isḥāq mentions that the Prophet ﷺ showed Rukānah a similar sign regarding a tree. He called it and it came until it stood in front of him, then he said: "Return", and it did so.[196]

Al-Ḥasan relates that the Prophet ﷺ expressed to his Lord that his people were causing him concern, and asked for a sign that would show him there was nothing to fear. Allah revealed to him to go to a certain wadi which contained a tree, and to call one of its branches. The Prophet ﷺ did so and the tree came, leaving its trace on the earth until it stood in front of him. The Prophet ﷺ detained it for as long as Allah wished and then said: "Go back as you came", and the tree returned. He said: "My Lord! I know that I have nothing to fear."[197] The same story is recorded by Ibn ʿUmar.[198]

Ibn ʿAbbās remembers that the Prophet ﷺ said to a Bedouin man: "If I summon a bunch of dates from this palm tree, will you testify that I am the Messenger of Allah?" The man replied that he would. It came bounding towards the Prophet ﷺ as soon as he called it. Then he told the tree to go back to its place, and it did.[199]

The Yearning of the Palm Trunk

The hadith concerning the moaning of the tree trunk adds further weight to the topic previously discussed. It is a famous hadith, and has been narrated with multiple chains of transmission. The following ten

---

196 Reported by Bayhaqī and Abū Nuʿaym from Abū Umāmah in *Al-Manāhil*, p. 583.

197 A *mursal* hadith. Reported by Bayhaqī, and Yunus ibn Bukayr in his additions to *Al-Sīrah* of Ibn Isḥāq, p. 279.

198 Reported by Bazzār (2410), Abū Yaʿlā (215), and others. Also mentioned by Haythamī in *Majmaʿ al-Zawā'id* (9/10), and Suyūṭī in *Manāhil al-Ṣafā*. Ibn Kathīr quotes the hadith in *Shamā'il al-Rasūl*, p. 235.

199 Reported by Tirmidhī (3628), Abū Yaʿlā (2350), and others. It was graded as authentic by Ibn Ḥibbān in *Mawārid*. Also authenticated by Ḥākim (2/620), and Dhahabī concurred.

Companions agreed on the meaning of this hadith: Ubayy ibn Ka'b,[200] Jābir ibn 'Abdullāh,[201] Anas ibn Mālik,[202] 'Abdullāh ibn 'Umar,[203] 'Abdullāh ibn 'Abbas,[204] Sahl ibn Sa'd,[205] Abū Sa'īd al-Khudrī,[206] Buraydah,[207] Umm Salamah,[208] and al-Muṭṭalib ibn Abī Wadā'a.[209]

Jābir ibn 'Abdullāh said: "The mosque was constructed from date palm trunks and topped with a roof. When the Prophet ﷺ addressed the people, he would lean against one of the trunks. When a minbar was built for him [to address people from], we heard that same trunk emitting a sound like a heavily-pregnant camel." Anas adds that the sound continued "until the mosque shook with its groans". According to Sahl, "people were crying at what they saw." In the narrations of al-Muṭṭalib and Ubayy, the trunk continued to moan "until it almost cracked and split open, before the Prophet ﷺ came and placed his hand on the trunk, and then it was silent."

In another version of the hadith, the Prophet ﷺ said: "This moaning

200 Reported by Ibn Mājah (1414), Aḥmad (5/137), and Dārimī (26).

201 Reported by Bukhārī (918).

202 Reported by Tirmidhī (3627), Ibn Mājah (1415), Abū Ya'lā (2756), and others. It was graded as authentic by Ibn Khuzaymah (1777), and Tirmidhī.

203 Reported by Bukhārī (3583).

204 Reported by Ibn Mājah (1415), Dārimī (39), and others. Its chain of transmission was authenticated by Būṣīrī in *Al-Zawā'id*, and Ibn Kathīr mentioned in *Shamā'il al-Rasūl*, p. 241: "Its chain of transmission agrees with the conditions of Muslim."

205 Reported by Dārimī (41), and its chain of transmission is weak. Ibn Kathīr mentions in *Shamā'il al-Rasūl*, p. 246, from the hadith of Ibn Abī Shaybah: "Its origins lie in Bukhārī and Muslim, and its chain of transmission agrees with their conditions." The hadith he is referring to is found in Bukhārī (377) and Muslim (544): it describes the construction of the minbar, without mentioning al-Ḥunayn.

206 Reported by Abū Ya'lā (1067), and Dārimī (38). Haythamī says in *Majma' al-Zawā'id* (2/180-181): "Its chain of transmission contains Mujālid ibn Sa'īd; some said he was reliable, and others said he was weak.

207 Reported by Dārimī (32), and its chain of transmission is weak.

208 Haythamī says in *Majma' al-Zawā'id* (2/181-182): "It was reported by Ṭabarānī in *Al-Kabīr*, and its narrators are authentic." It is mentioned by Ibn Kathīr in *Shamā'il al-Rasūl*, p. 250, from the hadith of Abū Nu'aym.

209 Būṣīrī attributed the hadith to al-Zubayr ibn Bakkār in *Al-Manāhil*, p. 587.

is for the remembrance (*dhikr*) it has lost."[210] Another narrator added: "I swear by the One with my soul in His hand, if the Prophet ﷺ had not embraced the trunk, it would have continued to moan until the Day of Judgement, out of sadness and longing for him. The Prophet ﷺ instructed for it to be buried under the minbar."[211] One of the transmissions from Sahl states: "It was buried under the minbar, or inserted into the roof"; and similar was related in the hadiths of al-Muṭṭalib, Sahl ibn Saʿd, and Isḥāq[212], all taken from Anas.

Ubayy mentions that the Prophet ﷺ used to pray in the direction of this particular trunk. When the mosque was dismantled, Ubayy took it. The trunk remained with him until it was consumed by the earth and returned to dust.

Al-Isfarāyīnī remembers an occasion when the Prophet ﷺ called the trunk over. It came, pulling up earth on the way, and he embraced it. Then he told it to return to its place, so it went back. In the hadith of Buraydah, the Prophet ﷺ said: "If you like, I can return you to the garden you came from; your roots can grow, your form can be completed, and your leaves and fruits can be replenished. Or, if you like, I can plant you in the Garden of Paradise, and the people with Allah can eat from your fruits. The Prophet ﷺ listened to hear its response. The trunk replied: "Plant me in the Garden of Paradise – a place where I will not decay – and the people with Allah can eat from my fruits." The Prophet ﷺ said: "I have done so. It has chosen the Permanent Abode over the temporary abode."

Al-Ḥasan would cry when he heard this story, and say: "Slaves of Allah! The wood yearned for the Messenger of Allah ﷺ, longing to join him

---

210 Reported by Aḥmad (3/300) from the hadith of Jābir ibn ʿAbdullāh. Ibn Khuzaymah provides a commentary in his *Ṣaḥīḥ* (1777), and a similar hadith was reported by Bukhārī (3584).

211 Taken from the hadith of Anas.

212 He is Isḥāq ibn Abī Ṭalḥah, a reliable man from the Followers who is narrated from in the six authentic collections of hadith. He died in 132 AH, or thereabouts.

in his position. You are the ones who should be longing to meet him!"[213]

The hadith was related from Jābir by: Ḥafṣ ibn ʿUbaydullāh (his name is also cited as ʿUbaydullāh ibn Ḥafṣ), Ayman, Abū Naḍrah, Ibn al-Musayyib, Saʿīd ibn Abī Karib, Kurayb, Abū Ṣāliḥ, Abū al-Zubayr, and Abū Salamah ibn ʿAbd al-Raḥmān ibn ʿAwf.[214] It was related from Anas ibn Mālik by: al-Ḥasan, Thābit, and Isḥāq ibn Abī Ṭalḥah. Nāfiʿ and Abū Ḥayyah narrated it from Ibn ʿUmar. Abū Naḍrah and Abū al-Waddāk narrated it from Abū Saʿīd. ʿAmmār ibn Abī ʿAmmār took the hadith from Ibn ʿAbbās. It was narrated from Sahl ibn Saʿīd by Abū Ḥāzim and ʿAbbās ibn Sahl. Kathīr ibn Zayd related from al-Muṭṭalib. ʿAbdullāh ibn Buraydah narrated the hadith from his father, and al-Ṭufayl ibn Ubayy did the same.

As you can see, this hadith was passed down by the people of authenticity. Not only was it narrated by the Companions above, but also many Followers – and others after them – whom we have not mentioned. Its wisdom has been transmitted to those who study the topic at hand. Above all, Allah is the One who establishes us on the right path.

Other Miracles Related to Inanimate Objects

It was narrated from Abū ʿAbdullāh Muhammad ibn ʿĪsā al-Tamīmī, from Abū ʿAbdullāh Muhammad ibn al-Murābiṭ, from al-Muhallab Abū al-Qāsim[215], from Abū al-Ḥasan al-Qābisī, from al-Marwaziyy, from al-Farabrī, from Bukhārī, from Muhammad ibn al-Muthannā, from Abū Aḥmad al-Zubayrī, from Isrāʾīl, from Manṣūr, from Ibrāhīm, from ʿAlqamah, from ʿAbdullāh ibn Masʿūd: "We used to hear food glorifying its

213 Taken from the narration of al-Ḥasan al-Baṣrī, from Anas.

214 It was also related from Jābir by Abū al-Zubayr, and Abū Salamah ibn ʿAbd al-Raḥmān ibn ʿAwf. Our esteemed teacher Ḥusayn Asad collated the chains of narration in the *Musnad* of Abū Yaʿlā (2756).

215 He was al-Muhallab ibn Aḥmad al-Andalūsī; he died in 435 AH. See the description of Dhahabī in *Siyar Aʿlām al-Nubalāʾ* (17/579).

Lord as it was being eaten."[216] In another wording: "We were eating with the Messenger of Allah ﷺ and we could hear the food glorifying its Lord."[217]

Anas reported: "The Prophet ﷺ took a handful of pebbles, and we heard them from his hand, glorifying Allah. Then he passed them to Abū Bakr, and they continued to glorify Allah. Then they were passed to us, and they stopped."[218] Abū Dharr related a similar hadith, and mentioned that the stones also continued to glorify when they were passed to ʿUmar and ʿUthmān.[219]

ʿAlī said: "We were in Makkah with the Messenger of Allah ﷺ. He went out to some of the surrounding areas, and every tree and mountain he passed greeted him with: 'May peace be upon you, Messenger of Allah!'"[220] Jabīr ibn Samurah recalls that the Prophet ﷺ said: "I know a stone in Makkah that used to greet me."[221] It has been said that this was referring to the Black Stone. According to ʿĀ'ishah, he said: "After Jibrīl came to me with the revelation, every stone or tree that I passed would greet me with: "May peace be upon you, Messenger of Allah!'"[222] Jābir ibn ʿAbdullāh said that every tree or stone the Prophet ﷺ passed would prostrate to him.[223]

---

216 The author took this hadith from the transmission of Bukhārī (3579).

217 Reported and authenticated by Tirmidhī (3633).

218 Suyūṭī attributes the hadith to Ibn ʿAsākir in *Manāhil al-Ṣafā* (589).

219 Reported by al-Zubayr (3/135). It was mentioned by Haythamī in *Majmaʿ al-Zawā'id* (5/179) and (8/299). In the first mention, he said: "It was related by Ṭabarānī in *Al-Muʿjam al-Awsaṭ*, and the chain of transmission contained Muhammad ibn Ḥamīd, who was a weak narrator." In the second mention, Haythamī said: "It was related by al-Zubayr with two chains of transmission; one of them consisted of reliable narrators."

220 Reported by Tirmidhī (3626), and Dārimī (21).

221 Reported by Muslim (2277).

222 Reported by Bazzār (2373). Haythamī said in *Majmaʿ al-Zawā'id* (8/259-260): "It was related by Bazzār from his teacher, ʿAbdullāh ibn Shabīb, who was a weak narrator."

223 Reported by Bayhaqī in *Al-Dalā'il*, and *Manāhil al-Ṣafā* (594).

In the hadith of al-ʿAbbās, the Prophet ﷺ wrapped him and his children in a cloak, and prayed that they would be shielded from the Hellfire just as they were shielded in the cloak. The door-frames and the walls of the house could be heard seconding the supplications: "Āmīn, āmīn."

Jaʿfar ibn Muhammad narrated from his father that the Prophet ﷺ was unwell, so Jibrīl came to him with a plate of pomegranate and grapes. The Prophet ﷺ ate from it, and the fruit glorified Allah.

Anas relates: "The Prophet ﷺ climbed Mount Uḥud with Abū Bakr, ʿUmar, and ʿUthmān. The mountain shook, so the Prophet ﷺ said: 'Be firm, Uḥud! You have upon you a Prophet, a truthful one (*siddīq*) and two martyrs.'"[224] A similar story about the cave of Ḥirā' is reported from Abū Hurayrah, who added that ʿAlī, Ṭalḥah and Zubayr were also present, and that the Prophet ﷺ said: "There is no-one upon you except a Prophet, a *siddīq*, or a martyr."[225] ʿUthmān says that the Prophet ﷺ was accompanied by ten Companions at Ḥirā', and that he was one of them. ʿUthmān also added the names of ʿAbd al-Raḥmān and Saʿd saying, "I forgot two names."[226] Saʿīd ibn Zayd recorded a similar hadith, again mentioning ten Companions, and adding himself.[227]

When the Quraysh were pursuing the Prophet ﷺ, the Thabīr mountain said to him: "Get down, Messenger of Allah! I am fearful that they will kill you upon me, and that Allah will punish me for that." The cave of Ḥirā' said: "Come to me, Messenger of Allah!"[228]

Ibn ʿUmar relates the Prophet ﷺ was on the minbar, and he recited: "And they have not shown Allah His proper reverence"[229] Then he said:

---

224 Reported by Bukhārī (3675).

225 Reported by Muslim (2417).

226 Reported by Tirmidhī (3699), Nasā'ī (6/236), and Ibn Abī ʿĀṣim al-Ḍaḥḥāk in *Al-Sunnah* (1447).

227 Reported by Abū Dāwūd (4648, 4649, 4650), Tirmidhī (3757), and Ibn Mājah (134).

228 Mentioned by Suyūṭī in *Manāhil al-Ṣafā* (601) without mentioning the narrator.

229 al-Anʿām, 91.

"The All-Compelling praises and glorifies Himself: 'I am the All-Compelling, I am the All-Compelling, I am the Grand, the Supreme.' The minbar shook until we thought the Prophet ﷺ would fall."[230]

Ibn ʿAbbās said that there were three hundred and sixty idols surrounding the Kaaba, with their legs set in stone and reinforced with lead. When the Prophet ﷺ entered the mosque, in the year that Makkah was liberated, he began pointing at them with a stick but without touching them, and he recited: "And declare, 'The truth has come and falsehood has vanished. Indeed, falsehood is bound to vanish.'"[231] Whenever he pointed at the face of an idol, it would fall on its back, and whenever he pointed at its back, it would fall on its face, until not a single idol remained.[232] A similar hadith was narrated from Ibn Masʿūd,[233] who said that the Prophet ﷺ was stabbing at the idols, and reciting: "Say, 'The truth has come, and falsehood will vanish, never to return.'"[234]

There was the monk whom the Prophet ﷺ met at a young age whilst travelling for trade with his uncle.[235] This monk would usually never come out for anyone but, on this occasion, he came out and mingled with them until he took the hand of the Messenger of Allah ﷺ, and said: "This is the leader of the whole word, and Allah will send him as a mercy." The elders of the Quraysh asked the monk how he knew. He replied: "Every tree and stone falls in prostration to him, and they only prostrate to a Prophet." The

230 Reported with this wording by Aḥmad (2/72). Similar was reported by Bukhārī (7412) and Muslim (2788/25).

231 *al-Isrā'*, 81.

232 Haythamī said in *Majmaʿ al-Zawā'id* (6/176): "It was reported by Ṭabarānī from reliable narrators, and by Bazzār in an abbreviated form."

233 Reported by Bukhārī (4287) and Muslim (1781).

234 *Saba'*, 49.

235 Reported by Tirmidhī (3620); and Bayhaqī in *Al-Dalā'il*, from the hadith of Abū Mūsā al-Ashʿarī. It was authenticated by Ḥākim in *Al-Mustadrak* (2/616), Ibn Ḥajr, and others. Tirmidhī praised the hadith, but others took an opposing view; see *Siyar A'lām al-Nubalā'* (4/533).

hadith continues: “The Prophet arrived with a cloud shading him. Whenever he came to a group of a people, he found that they had beaten him to the shade of a tree. When he sat down, the shadow of the tree moved to shade him.”

Miraculous Signs Related to Animals

It was narrated from Sirāj ibn ʿAbd al-Malik, also known as Abū al-Ḥusayn al-Ḥāfiẓ, from his father, from al-Qāḍī Yūnus, from Abū al-Faḍl al-Ṣaqallī, from Thābit ibn Qāsim ibn Thābit, from his father and grandfather, from Abū al-ʿAlāʾ Aḥmad ibn ʿImrān, from Muhammad ibn Faḍīl, from Yūnus ibn ʿAmr, from Mujāhid, that ʿĀʾishah said: “We had a domesticated animal. If the Messenger of Allah ﷺ was there, it would stay in its place, and when he left, it would run about.”[236]

ʿUmar related that the Messenger of Allah ﷺ was with a group of the Companions when a Bedouin man arrived who had caught a lizard. The man asked: “Who are you?” He replied: “The Prophet of Allah.” The man said: “I swear by al-Lāt and al-ʿUzzā, I do not believe in you, and neither does this lizard.” He threw it in front of the Prophet ﷺ, who called out to it. The lizard replied in a clear voice that everyone heard: “O adornment of the One who will establish the Day of Judgement, I am at your service!” The Prophet ﷺ said: “Who do you worship?” It replied: “The One whose Throne is in the sky, and whose Authority is in the earth, whose Path is in the ocean, and whose Mercy is in Paradise, and whose Punishment is in the Hellfire.” The Prophet ﷺ said: “Who am I?” The lizard replied: “The Messenger of the Lord of the Worlds, and the Seal of the Prophets.

---

236 Reported by Aḥmad (6/112, 150, 209), Abū Yaʿlā (4441, 4660). Ibn Kathīr commented in *Shamāʾil al-Rasūl*, p. 280: “This chain of transmission [of Aḥmad] conforms to the conditions of authenticity.” Haythamī says in *Majmaʿ al-Zawāʾid* (9/3-4): “It was related by Aḥmad, Abū Yaʿlā, al-Zubayr, Ṭabarānī in *Al-Awsaṭ*, and the narrators of Aḥmad are people of authenticity.” The hadith was also authenticated by Suyūṭī in *Manāhil al-Ṣafā* (605).

Whoever believes in you has succeeded, and whoever denies you has lost." After that, the Bedouin man embraced Islam.[237]

There is also the famous story of Abū Sa'īd al-Khudrī, about the wolf that spoke: A shepherd was herding his flock when a wolf made for one of the lambs. When the shepherd grabbed the lamb, the wolf sat down and said: "Do you not fear Allah? You have come between me and my provision!" The shepherd said, in amazement: "How can a wolf talk with the speech of human beings?" The wolf said: "Shall I tell you about something even more extraordinary? The Messenger of Allah ﷺ between two pieces of scorched, rocky land, telling people news of the past." The shepherd came to the Prophet ﷺ and told him what had happened. The Prophet ﷺ replied: "Stand up and tell the people", before adding, "He spoke the truth."[238] In some of the narrations of this hadith from Abū Hurayrah, the wolf said: "You are more extraordinary standing there with your sheep, and leaving the Prophet that Allah loves and values the most. The doors of Paradise have been opened for him, and its people see the struggle of his Companions. Nothing stands between you and him except for this ravine. Go, and join the soldiers of Allah!" The shepherd asked: "Who will look after my sheep?" The wolf said that he would look after them until the shepherd returned, so he left them in the care of the wolf and left. When he found the Prophet ﷺ in battle, he told him what had happened.

---

237 Haythamī says in *Majma' al-Zawā'id* (8/292-294): "It was related by Ṭabarānī in *Al-Ṣaghīr* and *Al-Awsaṭ*, from his teacher Muhammad ibn 'Alī ibn al-Walīd al-Baṣrī." Bayhaqī said the narrators are reliable. Ibn Diḥyah said: "The hadith about the lizard is fabricated (*mawḍū'*)." Dhahabī said, in *Al-Mīzān*: "It is a false report." Al-Mizzī said: "Neither the chain of transmission or the text are authentic." Al-Ḥawt al-Bayrūtī said in *Asnā al-Muṭālib*, p. 288: "It is a lie that has been fabricated against the Prophet ﷺ." See also: Ibn Kathīr, *Shamā'il al-Rasūl*, p. 285.

238 Reported by Aḥmad (3/83-84), Yunus ibn Bukayr in his additions to the *Sīrah* of Ibn Isḥāq, pp. 279-280, and others. Ibn Kathīr mentions in *Shamā'il al-Rasūl*, p. 274: "This chain of transmission conforms to the conditions of authenticity, and it was authenticated Bayhaqī." It was authenticated by Ibn Ḥibbān in *Mawārid al-Ẓam'ān* (2109). Also authenticated by Ḥākim (4/468), and Dhahabī concurred.

The Prophet ﷺ said: "Go back, and you will find all your sheep." On his return, the shepherd found his entire herd still present, and he slaughtered one lamb for the wolf.[239] Uhbān ibn Anas was the one who originally told the story, and the person the wolf spoke to.[240] It is also attributed to Salamah ibn ʿAmr ibn al-Akwaʿ, who said that it was the reason he became Muslim.[241]

Ibn Wahb relates something similar that happened to Abū Sufyān ibn Ḥarb and Ṣafwān ibn Umayyah: They saw a wolf which had captured a gazelle. The gazelle got away and entered the Sacred Mosque, and the wolf left it. The two men were stunned. The wolf spoke: "More amazing than what you have just seen is that Muhammed ibn ʿAbdullāh is in Madinah calling you to Paradise, and you are calling him to the Hellfire." Abū Sufyān replied: "I swear by al-Lāt and al-ʿUzzā, if you had said this in Makkah, the city would have been abandoned."[242]

ʿAbbās ibn Mirdās remembers being amazed by [what he thought was] the speech of a stone idol of his named Ḍimār, and its enchanting poetry which mentioned the Prophet ﷺ. A bird swooped down and said: "ʿAbbās! Are you amazed at the words of Ḍimār, but not amazed at your own situation? The Prophet ﷺ is calling you to Islam, and you are just sitting here!" These words inspired him to embrace the religion.[243]

---

239 Reported by Aḥmad (2/306), Maʿmar ibn Rāshid in *Al-Jāmiʿ* (11/383-384), and others. Haythamī said in *Majmaʿ al-Zawāʾid* (8/291-292): "It was reported by Aḥmad with reliable narrators, and by Bukhārī and Muslim in an abbreviated form." Haythamī was referring to Bukhārī (3690) and Muslim (2388). Mentioned by Suyūṭī in *Manāhil al-Ṣafā* (608).

240 Reported by Bukhārī in *Al-Tārīkh*, and Bayhaqī in *Al-Dalāʾil*. Bukhārī said that its chain of transmission lacked authority, due to the inclusion of ʿAbdullāh ibn ʿĀmir al-Aslamī, who was a weak narrator.

241 Mentioned by Suyūṭī in *Manāhil al-Ṣafā* (610), without mentioning the narrator.

242 Mentioned by Ibn Kathīr in *Shamāʾil al-Rasūl*, p. 280.

243 Suyūṭī said in *Al-Manāhil*: "Although I did not come across the hadith in this form, it was reported by Ṭabarānī in *Muʿjam al-Kabīr* in a similar wording, with an acceptable chain of transmission. The hadith of Ṭabarānī was mentioned by Haythamī in *Majmaʿ al-Zawāʾid* (8/246-247), where he said: "The chain of transmission contained ʿAbdullāh ibn ʿAbd al-ʿAzīz al-Laythī, who was declared

Jābir ibn ʿAbdullāh recalls a man coming to the Prophet ﷺ and accepting Islam, whilst they were besieging some of the fortresses of Khaybar. The man was herding the sheep for the people of Khaybar[244] and he said: "Messenger of Allah! What shall I do with them?" The Prophet ﷺ said: "Throw stones in their faces. Allah will fulfil your undertaking and return the sheep to their owners." He did so, and the entire flock went back to their people.[245]

Anas narrates that the Prophet ﷺ, Abū Bakr, ʿUmar, and a man from the Anṣār all entered a garden belonging to another person from the Anṣār. There were some sheep in the garden and they prostrated to the Prophet ﷺ. Abū Bakr said: "We are more duty-bound to prostrate to you than them."[246]

Abū Hurayrah mentions, similarly, when a camel prostrated to the Prophet ﷺ.[247] The story about the camel is also narrated by Thaʿlabah ibn Mālik[248], Jābir ibn ʿAbdullāh[249], Yaʿlā ibn Murrah[250], and ʿAbdullāh ibn

---

to be weak by the majority, but considered reliable by Saʿīd ibn Manṣūr."

244 A well-known town located 165 kilometres north of Madinah, on the route towards Syria.

245 Reported by Bayhaqī in *Al-Dalā'il*, and *Al-Manāhil,* p. 613.

246 Mentioned by Ibn Kathīr in *Shamā'il al-Rasūl*, p. 273; he said: "This hadith is *gharīb*, and there are unknown narrators in the chain of transmission." Other hadiths which mention a camel prostrating were reported by Aḥmad (3/158-159), and Bazzār (2454). Haythamī says in *Majmaʿ al-Zawā'id* (9/7): It was reported by Aḥmad and Bazzār, and the narrators were reliable, except for Ḥafṣ, the nephew of Anas. Its chain of narration was authenticated by Suyūṭī in *Al-Manāhil al-Ṣafā* (614), and praised by Ibn Kathīr in *Shamā'il al-Rasūl*, p. 259.

247 Reported by Bazzār (2451), and ʿAbdullāh ibn Ḥāmid in *Dalā'il al-Nubuwwah,* as it was found in *Shamā'il al-Rasūl,* p. 261. Haythamī said in *Majmaʿ al-Zawā'id* (9/7): "It was reported by Bazzār, and Tirmidhī, with a good chain of transmission." Suyūṭī agreed, in *Al-Manāhil,* p. 615.

248 Reported by Abū Nuʿaym in *Al-Dalā'il.*

249 Reported by Aḥmad (3/310), Dārimī (18), and others. Haythamī said in *Majmaʿ al-Zawā'id* (9/7): "It was related by Aḥmad with reliable narrators, although some of them were weak."

250 Reported by Aḥmad (4/170-172), and others. Graded as authentic by ʿIrāqī in *Takhrīj al-Iḥyā* (1/113). Also authenticated by Ḥākim (2/617-618), and Dhahabī concurred. Haythamī said in *Majmaʿ al-Zawā'id* (9/6): "It was related by Aḥmad and Ṭabarānī with two chains of narration, one of which was sound." See also: Ibn Kathīr, *Shamā'il al-Rasūl*, pp. 263-268.

Ja'far[251]. The camel would attack every person who entered the garden. When the Prophet ﷺ entered, it rested its lips on the ground. The Prophet ﷺ said: "There is nothing in the heavens and the earth that does not know I am the Messenger of Allah, except for rebellious jinn and human beings." The same was narrated by 'Abdullāh ibn Abī Awfā.

In another hadith about a camel, the Prophet ﷺ asked the people about its circumstances, and they informed him that they wished to slaughter it. An alternative wording records the Prophet ﷺ as saying: "It has complained about too much work, and too little feed." And, in another report: "It complained to me that after working it so hard from a young age, now you wish to slaughter it."

Al-Isfarāyīnī mentions in the story of al-Ghaḍbā', a female camel belonging to the Prophet ﷺ. The camel described her situation to the Prophet ﷺ. After that, she was the first to eat from the grass, and the wild predators would leave her and call out to her: "You belong to Muhammad!" After the Prophet ﷺ died, al-Ghaḍbā' refused to eat or drink, until she died too.

Ibn Wahb related: "The doves of Makkah shaded the Prophet ﷺ on the day of its liberation, and he supplicated for Allah to bless them."

Anas, Zayd ibn Arqam, and al-Mughīrah ibn Shu'bah narrated that the Prophet ﷺ said: "On the night of the cave[252] Allah commanded a tree, so it grew in my direction and shielded me. He also commanded two doves to stop at the entrance of the cave."[253] Another hadith says that a

---

251 Reported by Abū Dāwūd (2549), Aḥmad (1/204), and Nawawī in *Riyāḍ al-Ṣāliḥīn* (1009). Authenticated by Ḥākim (2/99-100), and Dhahabī agreed.

252 The night that the Messenger of Allah ﷺ and Abū Bakr took refuge in a cave after fleeing Makkah.

253 Reported by Bayhaqī in *Al-Dalā'il*, and Abū Nu'aym also in *Al-Dalā'il*. Haythamī said in *Majma' al-Zawā'id* (3/231): "It was related by Ṭabarānī in *Al-Kabīr*, Abū Muṣ'ab al-Makkī, and 'Awīn ibn 'Amr al-Qaysī, who related from him. The rest of the narrators are reliable."

spider wove its web in the mouth of the cave.[254] When the ones looking for them arrived at the cave, they said: "If there was anyone inside, then these two doves would not be at the mouth of the cave." The Prophet ﷺ heard what they said, and then they went away.

ʿAbdullāh ibn Qurṭ mentions an occasion when either five, six or seven sacrificial camels approached the Messenger of Allah ﷺ of their own accord, allowing him to slaughter them on the day of Eid.[255]

Umm Salamah narrates: "The Prophet ﷺ was in the desert when a gazelle called him: 'Messenger of Allah!' He replied: 'What is your need?' 'This Bedouin captured me', the gazelle answered, 'but I have two fawns on that mountain. Free me so that I can go and suckle them, and then I will come back.' The Prophet ﷺ asked for confirmation and the gazelle obliged, so they let it go and it returned as promised. The Prophet ﷺ tied it up again until the Bedouin man came back. He asked the Prophet ﷺ: 'Is there anything you need?' He replied: 'I request this gazelle.' The Prophet ﷺ freed the gazelle and it went bounding into the desert, calling: 'I bear witness that no-one is worthy of worship except Allah, and that you are the Messenger of Allah.'"[256]

When the Messenger of Allah sent his helper Safīnah to Muʿādh, who

---

254 Reported by Aḥmad (1/348) from the hadith of Ibn ʿAbbās. Ibn Kathīr said, in *Al-Sīrah* (2/239): "This chain is *ḥasan*, and it is the finest hadith regarding the story of the spider spinning its web in the mouth of the cave." Haythamī said in *Majmaʿ al-Zawāʾid* (7/27): "It was related by Aḥmad and Ṭabarānī, and the chains of transmission contained ʿUthmān ibn ʿAmr al-Juzrī, who was declared as reliable by Ibn Ḥibbān, but considered weak by others. The rest of the narrators were sound."

255 Reported by Abū Dāwūd (1765) and Aḥmad (4/350). Authenticated by Ḥākim (4/221), and Dhahabī concurred. Also presented by Suyūṭī in *Al-Jāmiʿ al-Ṣaghīr* (1061).

256 Haythamī said in *Majmaʿ al-Zawāʾid* (8/295): "It was related by Ṭabarānī, and the chain contains Aghlab ibn Tamīm, who was a weak narrator." Al-Mundhirī attests to the weakness of the hadith in *Al-Targhīb wa al-Tarhīb* (1/568). Sakhāwī said, in *Al-Maqāṣid al-Ḥasanah* (332): "The greeting of the gazelle has become famous amongst the people, and they included it in their praise of the Prophet ﷺ, but it is not from him in the first place, as Ibn Kathīr stated. Whoever attributes this story to the Prophet ﷺ has lied. However, the events have been described in several hadiths, which strengthen one another by their number." See also, *Shamāʾil al-Rasūl* (281-284).

was in Yemen, he came across a lion on the way. He informed the lion that he was the helper of the Messenger of Allah ﷺ, and carrying a message from him. The lion growled and moved off the path.[257] Another transmission states that Safīnah had accidentally gone astray from the route when he met the lion. He said: "I am the helper of the Messenger of Allah ﷺ", and the lion began nudging him with its shoulder until he was back on the right path.[258]

On another occasion, the Prophet ﷺ took hold of a lamb belonging to the ʿAbd al-Qays tribe by the ear. When he let go the impression of his fingers remained, and its offspring bore the same mark.[259]

There is also the donkey that was given to the Prophet ﷺ from the Battle of Khaybar, as recorded by Ibrāhīm ibn Ḥammād. The donkey told him: "My name is Yazīd ibn Shihāb", but the Prophet ﷺ renamed it Yaʿfūr. It would lead him to the houses of his Companions, knock on the door with its head, and call for them. When the Prophet ﷺ passed away, Yaʿfūr fell into a well, despondent and full of grief, and died.[260] Another hadith mentions a female camel that testified to the Prophet ﷺ that she had not been stolen by the person accompanying her but was, in fact, his property.[261]

---

257 Mentioned by Bukhārī in *Al-Tārīkh*. Reported by Maʿmar ibn Rāshid in *Al-Jāmiʿ* (20544), Baghawī (3732), and others.

258 Reported by Bazzār, and Bayhaqī. Ḥākim authenticated the hadith (2/619, 3/606), and Dhahabī concurred. Haythamī said in *Majma' al-Zawā'id* (9/369): "It was related by Bazzār and Ṭabarānī, both from trustworthy narrators."

259 Mentioned by Suyūṭī in *Al-Manāhil,* p. 623, without mentioning the narrator. Al-Khafājī said: "It is not known who narrated the hadith."

260 Mentioned by Ibn Ḥibbān in *Al-Majrūḥīn* (2/308), Ibn al-Jawzī in *Al-Mawḍūʿāt*, Ibn Kathīr in *Shamā'il al-Rasūl*, p. 288, and Ibn Ḥajr in *Al-Iṣābah* (4/186) from the hadith of Abū Manẓūr. Ibn Ḥibbān said: "This hadith has no origin." Ibn Kathīr said: "Many of the major scholars declared this hadith as *munkar*." Abū Mūsā al-Madīnī said: "This hadith is definitely *munkar*. It is not permissible for anyone to narrate it from me, unless they include my warnings against it." Al-Ḥawt al-Bayrūtī said in *Asnā al-Muṭālib*, p. 88: "It has not been established, and it is a fabricated hadith."

261 Reported by Ḥākim (2/619-620) from the hadith of Ibn ʿUmar. Ḥākim said: "The hadith is related by trustworthy narrators, but the chain also includes someone called Yaḥyā ibn ʿAbdullāh al-Maṣrī, who I am unfamiliar with." Dhahabī commented: "He is a liar, and he is the one who made

Ibn Qāni', and others, describe a goat that came to the Messenger of Allah ﷺ whilst he was with the army. The army, numbering approximately three hundred, had pitched in a place without water and were suffering from thirst. The Messenger of Allah ﷺ milked the goat and everyone drank until they were satisfied. Then he said to Rāfi': "What do you think about taking ownership of it?" So Rāfi' tied up the goat, but when he came back he found that it had run away. The Messenger of Allah ﷺ said: "Certainly, the One who brought it to you has taken it away."[262]

The Prophet ﷺ was once on a journey when the time for prayer arrived. He said to his horse: "Do not move – may Allah bless you – until we have completed our prayer", and turned it to face the direction for prayer (*qiblah*). The horse did not move a muscle until the Prophet ﷺ had prayed.[263]

Although not related to animals, we can also add the narration of al-Wāqidī: "The Prophet ﷺ sent out six messengers in one day, as emissaries to different kingdoms. Each one of them found that they spoke the language of the people they had been sent to."[264]

The hadiths related to this topic are extensive; we have picked the most famous, and those found in the books of leading scholars.

---

it up." The hadith was also reported by Ṭabarānī on the authority of Zayd ibn Thābit, with a chain that includes unknown narrators. Haythamī said in *Majma' al-Zawā'id* (9/11): "It includes narrators that I do not know."

262 Reported by Ibn Sa'd, Abū Aḥmad Ḥākim in *Al-Kunā*, Ibn Qāni', Ibn al-Sakan. Bayhaqī related it from the hadith of Nāfi', and the two of them shared a friendship. Ibn Kathīr said in *Shamā'il al-Rasūl*, p. 195: "This hadith is very strange, both in its text and its chain of transmission." Reported by Ibn 'Adiyy and Bayhaqī from the hadith of Sa'd, the helper of Abū Bakr. Ibn Kathīr said in *Shamā'il al-Rasūl*, p. 195: "This hadith is also very strange, both in its text and its chain of transmission, and the chain contains narrator whose circumstances are unknown." Haythamī said in *Majma' al-Zawā'id* (8/313): "It was related by Ṭabarānī, from trustworthy narrators."

263 Mentioned in *Al-Manāhil*, p. 627 without specifying the narrator.

264 Reported by Ibn Abī Shaybah in *Al-Muṣannaf* (14/328).

Bringing the Dead to Life, and the Speech of Infants

The author read the following hadith to Abū al-Walīd Hishām ibn Aḥmad al-Faqīh, Abū al-Walīd Muhammad ibn Rushd, Abū ʿAbdullāh Muhammad ibn ʿĪsā al-Tamīmī, and others: it was related to us from Abū ʿAlī al-Ḥāfiẓ, from Abū ʿUmar al-Ḥāfiẓ, from Abū Zayd, from ʿAbd al-Raḥmān ibn Yaḥyā, from Aḥmad ibn Saʿīd, from Ibn al-Aʿrābī, from Abū Dāwūd, from Wahb ibn Baqiyyah, from Khālid (al-Ṭaḥḥān), from Muhammad ibn ʿUmar, from Abū Salamah, that Abū Hurayrah said: "A Jewish lady presented the Prophet ﷺ with a roasted lamb at Khaybar, which she had poisoned. The Prophet ﷺ ate from it, and so did the people. Then he said: 'Everyone leave it, because the lamb has informed that it has been poisoned.' Bishr ibn al-Barāʾ died from eating the meat. The Prophet ﷺ asked the Jewish lady: 'What made you do this?' She replied: 'If you were a Prophet then it would not harm you. And if you were a king then I would have freed people from you.' He ordered for her to be killed."[265]

In the version recorded by Anas: "The Jewish lady said: 'I wanted to kill you.' The Prophet ﷺ replied: 'Allah did not allow you to overcome me.' We asked if we should kill her, but he declined."[266] The same was narrated by Abū Hurayrah from a chain of transmission without Wahb ibn Baqiyyah.[267] In the narration of Jābir ibn ʿAbdullāh, the Prophet ﷺ said: "This shoulder [of the lamb] informed me about the poison."[268] According to al-Ḥasan, he specified the thigh. Abū Salamah ibn ʿAbd al-Raḥmān

---

265 The chain of the author is found in Abū Dāwūd (4512), although he omits Abū Hurayrah. Reported by Ḥākim (3/219-220) from the narration of Abū Salamah, from Abū Hurayrah. Ḥākim said: "The hadith is authentic according to the conditions of Muslim", and Dhahabī concurred. The original source of the narration of Abū Hurayrah can be found in Bukhārī (3169).

266 Reported by Bukhārī (2617) and Muslim (2190).

267 Reported by Abū Dāwūd (4509) and Bayhaqī. See also Bukhārī (4249).

268 Reported by Abū Dāwūd (4510) from the chain of Ibn Shihāb. Abū Dāwūd said the chain was disconnected, but was supported by other hadiths on the topic.

reported that the lamb said: "I have been poisoned."[269] Ibn Isḥāq said that the Prophet ﷺ pardoned her.

Anas said: "I used to notice its effects on the lips of the Messenger of Allah ﷺ." Abū Hurayrah narrated that the Prophet ﷺ used to say, during his final illness: "The food from Khaybar still comes back to me. Right now, it is like it could cut my aorta."[270] Ibn Isḥāq noted that not only did Allah bless the Messenger ﷺ with Prophethood, but He bestowed upon him the honour of dying a martyr.

Ibn Suḥnūn[271] said: "The scholars of hadith agree that the Prophet ﷺ had the Jewish lady who poisoned him, killed." We have already mentioned the differing reports on this point. Ibn ʿAbbās stated that he gave her over to the family of Bishr ibn al-Barāʾ, and they killed her.[272]

There are also differing reports regarding the fate of the man who performed magic on the Prophet ﷺ. Al-Wāqidī said: "We consider the stronger opinion to be that he was forgiven, although in some reports it was related that he was killed."

The hadith about the poisoned lamb was also reported by al-Bazzār, from Abū Saʿīd. He gave a similar wording, except that he added to the end: "The Prophet ﷺ opened his hand and said 'eat, in the name of Allah.' We mentioned the name of Allah before we ate, and not one of us was harmed."[273] This hadith is well-known amongst the people, and has been

---

269 Reported by Abū Dāwūd (4512) from the hadith of Abū Salamah ibn ʿAbd al-Raḥmān. A *mursal* hadith.

270 Attributed to Ibn Saʿd in *Al-Manāhil,* p. 632. Reported by Abū Dāwūd (4512) from the hadith of Abū Salamah ibn ʿAbd al-Raḥmān, and he did not mention Abū Hurayrah. Bukhārī (4428) joined it with the narration of ʿĀʾishah.

271 He is ʿAbd al-Salām Suḥnūn al-Tanūkhī, from modern-day Tunisia, but at that time known as part of al-Maghrib; a great scholar of his generation and a jurist. He was born in 202 AH, and died in 256 AH. His biography and list of works can be found in *Siyar Aʿlām al-Nubalāʾ* (13/60-63)

272 Related by Ibn Saʿd. See *Al-Manāhil,* p. 634.

273 Reported by Bazzār (2424). Haythamī said in *Majmaʿ al-Zawāʾid* (8/295-296): "It was related by Bazzār from trustworthy narrators." The hadith was authenticated by Ḥākim (4/109), and Dhahabī

recorded by leading scholars in the field.

There is some difference of opinion on the nature of the speech itself; of the lamb, for example. Some say that Allah created the speech in the dead lamb – or the stone, or the tree – and that the letters and sounds originate from Him, and remain in their original form until they are heard. This was the position of Abū al-Ḥasan al-Ashʿarī and Abū Bakr al-Bāqillānī. Others propose that Allah gave these things life first, and then allowed them to speak. This second opinion was also attributed to Abū al-Ḥasan al-Ashʿarī. Both views are possible, and Allah knows best.

If we do not consider life as a precondition for letters and sounds to exist, then the first opinion is a possibility. If, however, we consider that speech cannot exist without life, then it is not. This was the stance of al-Jubbā'ī[274], that the words, letters and sounds of speech could not exist without a live being capable of producing them. Al-Jubbā'ī says that Allah Exalted gave them life, a mouth, and a tongue; i.e., the necessary tools to speak. This would apply to the stones, the date palm trunk, and the lamb shoulder. But if that had happened, it would have been recorded, and none of the narrators of hadith or Sīrah mention it. This points to a severe weakness in the claim. Above all, Allah is the One who gives success.

Wakīʿ relates from Fahd ibn ʿAṭiyyah, that the Prophet ﷺ was brought a child who had grown up without ever speaking. The Prophet ﷺ said to the child: "Who am I?" and he replied: "The Messenger of Allah."[275] Muʿarriḍ ibn Muʿayqīb narrated the same story, except that he said the child had just been born. The child was named Mubārak al-Yamāmah. The hadith is also known by the name of Shāṣūnah, who was one of the

concurred. Ibn Ḥajr declared the hadith as unacceptable (*munkar*) as is found *Manāhil al-Ṣafā* (635). See also, *Tuḥfat al-Dhākirīn*, p. 226.

274 He was Muhammad ibn ʿAbd al-Wahhāb al-Baṣrī al-Jubbā'ī, one of the Muʿtazilites. He died in Basra in 303 AH, at the age of 68. His biography can be found in *Siyar A'lām al-Nubalā'* (14/183).

275 Related by Bayhaqī from Shimr ibn ʿIṭiyyah, from some of his teachers. See *Al-Manāhil*, p. 833.

narrators in its chain of transmission. He relates the Prophet ﷺ replying to the child: "You have spoken the truth. May Allah bless you." This event took place in Makkah, during the Farewell Hajj. After that day, Mubārak did not speak again until he reached adulthood.[276]

Al-Ḥasan narrates: "A man came to the Prophet ﷺ and said that he had left his small daughter to die in a wadi. The Prophet ﷺ went with him to the wadi and called her by her name: 'Answer me by the permission of Allah Exalted!' The girl came out, saying: 'At your service!' The Prophet ﷺ said to her: 'Your parents have become Muslim, so, if you like, I can return you to them.' She replied: 'I have no need of them; I have found that Allah is better for me.'"[277]

Anas remembers a young man from the Anṣār passed away, and his mother was an old, blind woman. The people shrouded the young man and went to console his mother. She asked: "Has my son died?" They confirmed that he had. His mother cried: "Allah! If you know that I migrated for Your sake, and to be with Your Prophet, hoping that You would help me overcome every difficulty, then do not burden me with this affliction!" The moment we removed the veil covering his face, the young man was alive and joined us to eat.[278]

---

276 Reported by Ibn Qāni ʿ and Bayhaqī in *Al-Dalā'il*, Ibn al-Athīr in *Usd al-Ghābah*, and others, from the narration of Muhammad ibn Yunus al-Kudaymī, from Shāṣūnah ibn ʿUbayd, from Mu ʿarriḍ ibn ʿAbdullāh ibn Mu ʿarriḍ ibn Mu ʿayqīb, from his father, and then his grandfather, Mu ʿarriḍ ibn Mu ʿayqīb. Muhammad ibn Yunus al-Kudaymī is a weak narrator, as was mentioned by Ibn Kathīr in *Shamā'il*, p. 307. Ibn Ḥajr said in *Al-Iṣābah* (3/424): "Bayhaqī related the hadith from the chain of al-Kudaymī, who was an untrustworthy narrator. Mu ʿarriḍ, his father, and Shāṣūnah are all unknown." However, the hadith was also transmitted with chains other than that of al-Kudaymī: It was reported by Ibn Jumay ʿ in his *Mu'jam*, p. 354, no. 337, Bayhaqī in *Al-Dalā'il* (2/59-61), and al-Khaṭīb in *Tārīkh Baghdād*, Ḥākim in *Al-Iklīl*. Reported by Bayhaqī in *Al-Manāhil*. Ibn Kathīr said: "It was accepted by Suyūṭī in *Al-Khaṣā'is al-Kubrā*." Bayhaqī stated that the chain was *mursal*, and originated with the people of Kūfah. See also, *Lisān al-Mī*zān (5/198).

277 A *mursal* hadith.

278 Reported by Bayhaqī in *Al-Dalā'il*, from the chain of ʿĪsā ibn Yūnūs, from ʿAbdullāh ibn ʿAwn, from Anas. Ibn Kathīr said in *Al-Shamā'il al-Rasūl*, p. 564: "The narrators are reliable, but there is a break in the chain between ʿAbdullāh ibn ʿAwn and Anas, and Allah knows best." Also in *Al-*

ʿAbdullāh ibn ʿUbaydullāh al-Anṣārī recalls: "I was one of the group who buried Thābit ibn Qays ibn Shammās, who was killed in the Battle of Yamāmah. After we had put his body into the grave, we heard him calling: 'Muhammad is the Messenger of Allah. Abū Bakr is the truthful one. 'Umar is the martyr. 'Uthmān is the kind, merciful one.' We looked into the grave, but he was lifeless."[279]

Al-Nuʿmān ibn Bishr narrates that Zayd ibn Khārijah fell down dead in one of the streets of Madinah. His body was lifted up and shrouded. Between the prayers of *maghrib* and *'ishā'*, the women who were crying and grieving around him heard a voice, saying: "Be silent! Be silent!" They uncovered his face, and he continued: "Muhammad is the Messenger of Allah, the unlettered Prophet, and the Seal of the Prophets. That was recorded in the First Book. He told the truth, he told the truth." Then he mentioned Abū Bakr, ʿUmar, and ʿUthmān. Finally, he said: "May the peace, mercy and blessings of Allah be upon you, Messenger of Allah!" and he was lifeless once again.[280]

Healing Sick and Disabled People

There was a story from the Battle of Uḥud narrated by Abū al-Ḥasan from ʿAlī ibn Musharraf and others, from Abū Isḥāq al-Ḥabbāl, from Abū Muhammad ibn al-Nuḥās, from Ibn al-Ward, from al-Barqī, from Ibn Hishām, from Ziyād al-Bakkā'ī, from Muhammad ibn Isḥāq, from Ibn Shihāb and ʿĀṣim ibn ʿUmar ibn Qatādah, that Saʿīd ibn Abī Waqqāṣ

Shamā'il, Ibn al-Zamalkānī says, p. 563: "The wording was established from Anas." Ibn Kathīr also said: "It was related from Abū Bakr ibn Abī al-Dunyā and Abū Bakr al-Bayhaqī in a different form, from Ṣāliḥ ibn Bashīr al-Murrī, one of the pious men of Basra."

279 Reported by Bayhaqī in *Al-Dalā'il*. A similar hadith was reported by Ibn Kathīr in *Al-Shamā'il al-Rasūl*, p. 301, and he attributed it to Ibn Abī al-Dunyā.

280 Reported by Ṭabarānī, Abū Nuʿaym, Ibn Mandah, and Ibn Abī al-Dunyā, from the hadith of Anas ibn Mālik (see *Al-Manāhil*, 640). Ibn Kathīr said in *Al-Shamā'il*, p. 565: "As for the story of Zayd ibn Khārijah and his speech after he had died, it is well-established from many authentic sources."

said: "The Messenger of Allah ﷺ handed me an arrow without its arrowhead and said: 'Shoot it.'"[281]

That day, the Messenger of Allah ﷺ shot from his own bow until it split. During the battle, the eye of Qatādah ibn al-Nuʿmān was injured and left dangling from its socket. The Messenger of Allah ﷺ reinserted it, and from then on it became his best eye.[282] This story was related by Abū Saʿīd al-Khudrī,[283] ʿĀṣim ibn ʿUmar ibn Qatādah, and Yazīd ibn ʿIyāḍ.

During the expedition of Dhū Qarad[284], Abū Qatādah had been injured by an arrow, and the Prophet ﷺ spat on the wound on his face. Abū Qatādah said: "There was no throbbing or festering of the wound [after that]."[285]

Nasāʾī reported from ʿUthmān ibn Ḥunayf, that a blind man once said: "Messenger of Allah! Pray to Allah to restore my sight." The Prophet ﷺ told him: "Go and make *wuḍū'*, then perform two units of prayer (*rakʿatayn*), and then say: 'Allah! I ask You, and I turn to You, with Your Prophet Muhammad, the Prophet of Mercy. I turn to my Lord, asking Him to re-

---

281 The chain of the author is taken from Ibn Isḥāq, *Sīrah*, p. 322-328, and is originally from Bukhārī (4055) and Muslim (2412), with a different wording.

282 Reported by Ibn Isḥāq in his *Sīrah*, p. 328; and Bayhaqī in *Al-Dalā'il*, in a *mursal* hadith from ʿĀṣim ibn ʿAmr ibn Qatādah. The chain was connected by Abū Nuʿaym in *Al-Dalā'il*, from the narration of ʿĀṣim ibn ʿAmr ibn Qatādah from Muhammad ibn Lubayd, from Qatādah ibn al-Nuʿmān; and by Abū Yaʿlā (1549) from the narration of from ʿĀṣim ibn ʿAmr ibn Qatādah, from his father, from Qatādah ibn al-Nuʿmān. Suyūṭī said in *Al-Manāhil*: "Ibn ʿAdiyy and Bayhaqī connected the chain from ʿĀsim to his grandfather Qatādah." Haythamī said in *Majmaʿ al-Zawā'id* (8/297-298): "It was related by Ṭabarānī and Abū Yāʿlā. The chain of Ṭabarānī contains unknown narrators, and the chain of Abū Yaʿlā contains ʿAbd al-Ḥamīd al-Ḥammānī, who was a weak narrator." The story is also found in the *Mustadrak* of Ḥākim (3/255), without mentioning the chain. It is related by al-Aṣmaʿī (see *Tahdhīb al-Asmā' wa al-Lughāt*, 2/58) from Abū Maʿshar.

283 Attributed by Ibn Kathīr to Dāraquṭnī as a *gharīb* hadith, in *Al-Sīrah* (3/66); and by Suyūṭī to Bayhaqī, in *Al-Manāhil*, p. 642.

284 Qarad was a black mountain above the wadi of al-Nuqmā, about thirty-five kilometres northeast of Madinah.

285 Reported by Ḥākim (3/480); Bayhaqī in *Al-Dalā'il*; al-Wāqidī in *Al-Maghāzī* (2/545) from the hadith of Abū Qatādah al-Anṣārī (they differed as to whether his name was al-Ḥārith, ʿAmr, or al-Nuʿmān ibn Ribʿī). Al-Khafājī said, in *Nasīm al-Riyāḍ* (3/105): "The hadith is *ṣaḥīḥ* and was related by Tirmidhī and Bayhaqī. I did not find it in the *Sunan* of Tirmidhī, and Allah knows best."

move the veil from my eyes. Allah, allow him (i.e., the Prophet ﷺ) to intercede for me!'" When the man returned, Allah had restored his sight.[286]

Ibn Mulāʿib al-Asinnah was suffering from oedema (swelling caused by fluid retention), so he sent a messenger to the Prophet ﷺ. When he arrived, the Prophet ﷺ took a handful of dust from the ground, spat into it, and gave it to the messenger. He took it in astonishment, thinking he would be mocked, and returned. Ibn Mulāʿib was on his deathbed. He drank what the Prophet ﷺ had sent, and Allah cured him.[287]

Al-ʿUqaylī reported from Ḥabīb ibn Fudayk[288] that his father's eyes turned white, rendering him completely blind. The Prophet ﷺ spat onto his eyes, and his sight returned. He later saw his father threading a needle at the age of eighty.[289]

Kulthūm ibn al-Ḥuṣayn[290] was shot in the throat during the Battle of Uḥud. The Messenger of Allah ﷺ spat onto the lesion and it was healed.[291] He did the same for ʿAbdullāh ibn Unays, and prevented his wound from becoming infected.[292] During the Battle of Khaybar, he spat onto the eyes of ʿAlī; they had become inflamed, but afterwards were clear again.[293] In

---

286 Reported by Nasāʾī in *ʿAmal al-Yawm wa al-Laylah* (660), Tirmidhī (3578), Ibn Mājah (1385), Aḥmad (4/138), Ibn al-Sunnī in *ʿAmal al-Yawm wa al-Laylah* (628), and others. It was graded as authentic by Ḥākim (1/313, 519, 526), and Dhahabī concurred. It was also authenticated by Tirmidhī, Ibn Khuzaymah, Ṭabarānī, and others.

287 A *mursal* hadith. Suyūṭī said in *Al-Manāhil*: "It was related by al-Wāqidī (1/350), and Abū Nuʿaym in *Al-Dalāʾil* from the hadith of ʿUrwah, also known as ʿĀmir ibn Mālik. They differed about whether ʿĀmir ibn Mālik became Muslim, and his biography can be found in *Al-Iṣābah* of Ibn Ḥajr.

288 His name is also cited as Furayk or Fuwayk.

289 Reported by al-ʿUqaylī, Bayhaqī, Ibn Abī Shaybah, and Ṭabarānī. Haythamī said in *Majmaʿ al-Zawāʾid* (8/298): "It was related by Ṭabarānī with some narrators I do not know in the chain."

290 He is Abū Ruhm al-Ghifārī.

291 Mentioned by al-Wāqidī in *Al-Maghāzī* (1/243), and Ibn Ḥajr attributed it to Abū ʿUrwah in *Al-Iṣābah* (4/71).

292 Related by Ṭabarānī from the hadith of ʿAbdullāh ibn Unays. Haythamī said in *Majmaʿ al-Zawāʾid* (8/298): "The chain of transmission contains ʿAbd al-ʿAzīz ibn ʿImrān, who was a weak narrator."

293 Reported by Bukhārī (3701) and Muslim (2406), from Sahl ibn Saʿd al-Sāʿidī.

the same battle, Salamah ibn al-Akwaʿ was injured on the shin; the Prophet ﷺ blew onto the area and he was healed.[294] Zayd ibn Muʿādh was cut in the foot, by a sword strike intended for Kaʿb ibn al-Ashraf; again, the spit of the Prophet ﷺ treated him.[295] This was on the day that Ibn al-Ashraf was killed. During the Battle of al-Khandaq, ʿAlī ibn al-Ḥakam sustained damage to his leg. When the Prophet ﷺ spat on the area, it healed immediately, without the injured man even dismounting his horse.[296]

ʿAlī ibn Abī Ṭālib once complained of some pain and started to supplicate to Allah. The Prophet ﷺ prayed: "Allah! Heal him!" Then he struck ʿAlī with his foot, and he never complained of the pain again.[297]

During the Battle of Badr, Abū Jahl cut off the hand of Muʿādh ibn ʿAfrāʾ. He came to the Prophet ﷺ cradling his severed hand. The Prophet ﷺ spat on where it was cut, and the hand was reattached to his arm.[298] At the same battle, Khubayb ibn Yasāf suffered a strike to the neck that left half of it hanging loose. The Prophet ﷺ was with him at the time and continued to blow on his neck until he convalesced.[299]

The Prophet ﷺ was once approached by a woman from the tribe of Khathʿam. She had a child with her who was suffering from an impediment and could not speak. Some water was brought, and the Prophet ﷺ rinsed his mouth and washed his hands with it. Then he gave it to

---

294 Reported by Bukhārī (4206) from the hadith of Salamah ibn al-Akwaʿ.

295 Related by ʿAbd ibn Hamīd from ʿIkrimah in his *Tafsīr*. Also reported by al-Wāqidī and Bayhaqī.

296 Ibn Ḥajr attributes the narration to Baghawī, Ṭabarānī, Ibn al-Sakan, and Ibn Mandah, from the chain of Kathīr ibn Muʿāwiyah ibn al-Ḥakam al-Sulamī from his father. Ibn Ḥajr said: "The chain contains Ṣighār ibn Ḥamīd, an unknown narrator." Haythamī said in *Majmaʿ al-Zawāʾid* (8/298): "It was related by Ṭabarānī with some narrators I do not know in the chain. The chain also contains Yaʿqūb ibn Muhammad al-Zuhrī, who was declared weak by the majority, although Ibn Ḥibbān said he was reliable."

297 Reported by Tirmidhī (3564), and others. It was authenticated by Ḥākim (2/620), and Dhahabī concurred.

298 Related by Ibn Wahb.

299 Related by Ibn Isḥāq, and Bayhaqī reported from him in *Al-Manāhil*, p. 655.

the woman and told her to wipe the child and let him drink from it. The young boy was cured, and was blessed with an intelligence to outshine the brightest minds.[300] A similar story is narrated by Ibn ʿAbbās: "A woman came to the Prophet ﷺ with her son, who was either suffering from mental illness or being tormented by jinn. The Prophet ﷺ wiped over his chest; the boy vomited up what looked like a black capsule and was cured.[301]

A cooking pot flipped and fell on the arm of Muhammad ibn Ḥaṭib whilst he was a child. The Prophet ﷺ wiped over it and supplicated for him. Then he spat and it was healed immediately.[302]

Shuraḥbīl had a sore on his hand which was preventing him from gripping a sword or holding onto the reins of an animal. He complained about it to the Prophet ﷺ, who started massaging and pressing it with his hand, continuing until the sore had disappeared without a trace.[303]

A slave-girl once asked the Prophet ﷺ for some food whilst he was eating. He offered her what was in front of him, but the girl lacked modesty, and she said: "I want the food that is in your mouth." So, he took the food out of his mouth and gave it to her. Once asked, the Prophet ﷺ would never refuse a request. It was said that when that food reached the

---

300 Related by Ibn Abī Shaybah in *Al-Muṣannaf*, from Umm Jundub (see *Al-Manāhil*, p. 656).

301 Reported by Aḥmad (1/254), Dārimī (19), and others. Haythamī said in *Majmaʿ al-Zawāʾid* (9/2): "It was related by Aḥmad and Ṭabarānī. The chain includes Farqad al-Sabkhī, who was declared as reliable by Ibn Maʿīn and al-ʿAjalī, but considered weak by others."

302 Reported by Aḥmad (3/418) and others, from the hadith of Muhammad ibn Ḥāṭib, from his mother Umm Jamīl bint al-Mujallil. It was authenticated by Ibn Ḥibbān in *Mawārid* (1415). The story was originally recorded by Nasāʾī in ʿAmal al-*Yawm wa al-Laylah* (187, 1024, 1025, 1026), Aḥmad (3/418), and others, from the hadith of Muhammad ibn Ḥāṭib, and authenticated by Ibn Ḥibbān in *Mawārid* (1416). Haythamī said: "It was related by Aḥmad and Ṭabarānī. The narrators in the hadith of Aḥmad are sound."

303 Related by Ṭabarānī from the hadith of Muhammad ibn ʿUqbah ibn Shuraḥbīl, from his grandfather ʿAbd al-Raḥmān and then his great-grandfather after him. Haythamī said in *Majmaʿ al-Zawāʾid* (8/298): "It was related by Ṭabarānī. The narrators in the chain from Makhlad upwards are unknown to me, but the rest of them are sound."

girl's stomach, she began to feel a sense of shyness and became the most self-effacing woman in Madinah.[304]

The Supplications of the Prophet ﷺ Being Answered

This is an expansive topic, and it is well-established that the supplications and prayers of the Prophet ﷺ were answered. Ḥudhayfah said that when the Prophet ﷺ prayed for someone, whatever he had asked for would reach that person, their children and their grandchildren.[305]

Abū Muhammad al-ʿAttābī narrated, from Abū al-Qāsim Ḥātim ibn Muhammad, from Abū al-Ḥasan al-Qābisī, from Abū Zayd al-Marwaziyy, from Muhammad ibn Yūsuf, from Muhammad ibn Ismāʿīl, from ʿAbdullāh ibn Abī al-Aswad, from Ḥaramī, from Shuʿbah, from Qatādah, from Anas: "My mother said: 'Messenger of Allah! Take Anas as a helper! Pray to Allah for him!' The Prophet ﷺ supplicated: 'Allah! Give him an abundance of wealth and children and put blessings in what you give him.'"[306] As ʿIkrimah relates, Anas said: "I swear by Allah, I have an abundance of wealth, and my children and grandchildren add up to about one hundred!"[307] In another transmission, Anas adds: "I do not know anyone who has a more prosperous life than me. I have buried one hundred children with my own hands, and I am not speaking about grandchildren or miscarriages."[308]

The Prophet ﷺ also prayed for blessings for ʿAbd al-Raḥmān ibn

---

304 Related by Ṭabarānī from the hadith of Abū Umāmah. Haythamī said in *Majmaʿ al-Zawāʾid* (9/21): "Its chain is weak."

305 Reported by Aḥmad (5/385-386). Haythamī said in *Majmaʿ al-Zawāʾid* (8/368): "It was related by Aḥmad, from one of the sons of Ḥudhayfah – I do not know who he is – who took the hadith from his father."

306 The chain of the author is taken from Bukhārī (6344). It was also reported by Muslim (2481/142).

307 Reported by Muslim (2481/142).

308 Suyūṭī attributes this narration to Bayhaqī in *Al-Manāhil*, p. 661.

ʿAwf.[309] ʿAbd al-Raḥmān said: "Any time I lifted a stone I expected to find gold underneath, and Allah would open the way for me." When he died, people set to work on the gold he left behind with hatchets, until their hands were calloused and cramped. Each of his four wives inherited eighty thousand dirhams, and some said it was a hundred thousand. He was famous for philanthropy during his life, and followed it up with a bequest of fifty thousand dirhams after passing away. His generosity was renowned; freeing thirty slaves in a single day, and once giving away a trade caravan comprising seven hundred camels in charity. The caravan had been received by ʿAbd al-Raḥmān bearing all types of foods and treats; he donated not only the goods but the animals carrying them too.

The Prophet ﷺ prayed for Muʿāwiyah to be a firm fixture in the region, and he became Caliph.[310] He prayed for Allah to accept the supplications of Saʿd ibn Abī Waqqāṣ; after that, anything Saʿd asked for was answered.[311] The Prophet ﷺ supplicated for the religion of Islam to be elevated either through ʿUmar or Abū Jahl. Allah answered the supplication with ʿUmar.[312] Ibn Masʿūd once said: "We remain elevated and honoured since ʿUmar accepted Islam."[313] The people were suffering from thirst during one of the battles, and ʿUmar asked the Prophet ﷺ to supplicate. As soon as he did so, a cloud arrived, gave them the rain they needed, and then floated away. Once the Prophet ﷺ began to supplicate during the

---

309 Reported by Bukhārī (5155) and Muslim (1427).

310 Reported by Bayhaqī in *Al-Dalā'il* (6/446), and he said: "The narrator Ismāʿīl ibn Ibrāhīm is considered weak by the scholars of hadith, but this hadith is supported by other narrations." It was attributed to Ibn Saʿd in *Al-Manāhil*, p. 662.

311 Reported by Tirmidhī (3751) and declared as authentic by Ibn Ḥibbān (2215). Also authenticated by Ḥākim (3/499), and Dhahabī concurred.

312 Reported by Tirmidhī (3681), Aḥmad (2/95), and others, from the hadith of Ibn ʿUmar. Authenticated by Ibn Ḥibbān in *Mawārid* (2179). Tirmidhī said: "This hadith is *ḥasan ṣaḥīḥ gharīb*." Also reported by Tirmidhī (3683) from the hadith of Ibn ʿAbbās, and by Ḥākim (3/83) from the hadith of Ibn Masʿūd.

313 Reported by Bukhārī (3684).

prayer of *istisqā*'[314] and the rain began to fall. Then the people complained about the rain, so he supplicated again and the sky cleared.[315]

The Prophet ﷺ once said to Abū Qatādah: "May your face prosper! Allah, put blessings in his hair and his skin!" He died at the age of seventy, looking no older than fifteen.[316] The Prophet ﷺ prayed for al-Nābighah: "May Allah not shatter your jaw!" and he never lost a tooth after that.[317] Another transmission relates that he had the most beautiful front teeth; if one fell out, another would grow in its place. He lived to the age of 120, although some say he was older. The Prophet ﷺ supplicated for Ibn ʿAbbās: "Allah, give him understanding of the religion, and teach him its interpretation!"[318] He came to be known as the Scholar, and the Exegete of the Qur'an. The Prophet ﷺ prayed for ʿAbdullāh ibn Jaʿfar to be blessed in his business transactions.[319] He made a profit on every item he purchased. The Prophet ﷺ called on Allah to bless Miqdād, and he ended up with sacks of wealth.[320] He asked for the same for ʿUrwah ibn Abī al-Jaʿd,[321] who said: "I used to stay in al-Kunāsah[322], and when I returned, I had made forty thousand dirhams in profit." Bukhārī said that if ʿUrwah

---

314 A special prayer for rain, typically performed during times of drought.

315 Reported by Bukhārī (1016); Muslim (897) from the hadith of Anas ibn Mālik.

316 Reported by Ḥākim (3/480), and Bayhaqī in *Al-Dalāʾil*. See also, *Majmaʿ al-Zawāʾid* (9/319).

317 Reported by Bazzār (2104), Ibn al-Athīr in *Usd al-Ghābah*, Ibn Ḥajr in *Al-Iṣābah*, and others, from the hadith of al-Nābighah al-Jaʿdiyy. Haythamī said in *Majmaʿ al-Zawāʾid* (8/126): "It was related by Bazzār. The chain contains Yaʿlā ibn al-Ashdaq, who was a weak narrator." See *Al-Iṣābah* for the biography of al-Nābighah al-Jaʿdiyy.

318 Reported by Aḥmad (1/266, 314, 328) from the hadith of Ibn ʿAbbās. It was authenticated by Ḥākim (3/534), and Dhahabī concurred. Also found, with a different wording, in Bukhārī (143) and Muslim (2477).

319 Reported by Bayhaqī in *Al-Dalāʾil*, from the hadith of ʿAmr ibn Ḥurayth.

320 Reported by Bayhaqī in *Al-Dalāʾil*.

321 Reported by Bukhārī (3642) from the hadith of ʿUrwah ibn Abī al-Jaʿd al-Bāriqī himself.

322 An area in al-Kūfah, in Iraq.

bought dust, he would have made a profit.[323] A similar story is narrated about Gharqadah.[324]

There was an occasion when a female camel belonging to the Prophet ﷺ took off. He supplicated, and a powerful tornado carried it back to him. The Prophet ﷺ made *du'ā'* for the mother of Abū Hurayrah, and she became a Muslim.[325] He prayed for 'Alī to be protected from conditions that were extremely hot or icily cold. After that, 'Alī would wear winter clothes in the summer, and summer clothes in the winter, and never suffered from the hot or cold.[326] The Prophet ﷺ prayed to Allah that his daughter Fāṭimah would never feel hunger. She confirmed that she never got hungry again.[327] Al-Ṭufayl ibn 'Amr asked the Prophet ﷺ to give him a sign to show to his people. He called: "Allah, illuminate him!" Suddenly, a light shone from between the eyes of al-Ṭufayl. He said: "Lord! I am afraid that they will think it is a punishment." So, it was moved to the end of his whip; he would use it to brighten the way during the pitch-black of the night, and he became known as the Possessor of the Light.[328]

The Prophet ﷺ made *du'ā'* against the tribe of Muḍar and they went completely without rain, until the Quraysh managed to conciliate with him. He then supplicated for Muḍar and the rain returned.[329] When Khosrow, the King of Persia, ripped up a letter the Prophet ﷺ had sent him, he

---

323 Reported by Bukhārī (3642).

324 Reported by Ibn Qāni' from the hadith of Gharqadah (see *Al-Iṣābah*, 3/190). Al-Ḥāfiz said: "That is a mistake. It was from 'Urwah, not Gharqadah."

325 Reported by Muslim (2491) from the hadith of Abū Hurayrah.

326 Reported by Ibn Mājah (117) from the hadith of 'Alī. Būṣīrī said: "Its chain is weak."

327 Reported by Bayhaqī in *Al-Dalā'il*, from the hadith of 'Imrān ibn Ḥuṣayn.

328 Mentioned by Ibn Isḥāq without a chain (see also, the *Sīrah* of Ibn Hishām, 1/382). Related by Ṭabarī, and by 'Abd al-Barr in *Al-Istī'āb* from the transmission of Hishām ibn Muhammad ibn al-Sā'ib al-Kalbī.

329 Reported by Bukhārī (4821) and Muslim (2798/40) from the hadith of Ibn Mas'ūd.

prayed for Allah to tear apart their kingdom.[330] It disappeared without a trace, and the Persians had no authority anywhere in the world. There was a boy who cut out prayer, so the Prophet ﷺ made *du'ā'* for Allah to cut him off.[331] The boy was unable to walk or stand after that.

The Prophet ﷺ saw a man eating with his left hand, and said to him: "Eat with your right." The man replied: "I cannot." The Prophet ﷺ repeated: "You could not", and he never managed to lift that food to his mouth.[332] The Prophet ﷺ once said, concerning 'Utbah ibn Abī Lahab: "Allah, give one of your predators power over him."[333] He was eaten by a lion. There was a woman whom he told "may a lion eat you", and it happened.[334]

There is also the famous hadith narrated by 'Abdullāh ibn Mas'ūd, about when the Prophet ﷺ supplicated against the Quraysh, after a group of them had placed animal intestines covered in blood and excrement on the back of his neck whilst he was prostrating in prayer. The Prophet ﷺ individually named them in his *du'ā'*, and Ibn Mas'ūd said: "I saw every one of them killed at the Battle of Badr."[335] Al-Ḥakam ibn Abī al-'Āṣ used to twitch and wink in the presence of the Prophet ﷺ, making secretive gestures. The Prophet ﷺ saw him and said: "May you stay like that." He continued to twitch until the day he died.[336] The Proph-

---

330 Reported by Bukhārī (64) in a *mursal* hadith from Ibn al-Musayyib.

331 Reported by Abū Dāwūd (707) from the hadith of Sa'īd ibn Ghazwān, from his father. Its chain was declared as weak by Ibn al-Qaṭān, 'Abd al-Ḥaqq al-Ishbīlī, and Ibn Qayyim al-Jawziyyah. Dhahabī said: "I think it is fabricated."

332 Reported by Muslim (2021) from the hadith of Salamah ibn al-Akwa'.

333 Reported by Ḥākim (2/539) from the hadith of Nawfal ibn Abī 'Aqrab, from his father. Ḥākim said the hadith was authentic, and Dhahabī concurred. Mentioned by Ibn Kathīr in his *tafsīr* of Surah al-Najm, from the hadith of Ibn 'Asākir from Habbār ibn al-Aswad. See also, *Majma' al-Zawā'id* (6/18-19).

334 Reported by Ibn Sa'd in al-Ṭabaqāt, from the narration of al-Kalbī, from Abū Ṣāliḥ, from Ibn 'Abbās. The chain includes Muhammad ibn al-Sā'ib al-Kalbī, who was accused of lying in his narrations.

335 Reported by Bukhārī (240) and Muslim (1794).

336 Reported by Bayhaqī in *Al-Dalā'il.*

et ﷺ cursed Muḥallim ibn Jathāmah, and he was killed by a lion. They tried to bury him several times, but each time, the earth spat him out. Eventually, they had to throw his body into narrow ravine and cover it with rocks.[337] There was a man who falsely denied selling a horse to the Prophet ﷺ, when in fact he had. The Prophet ﷺ returned the horse, and said: "Allah! If he is lying, do not put any blessings in it!"[338] The horse's legs became heavy and stiff.

The prayers of the Prophet ﷺ that were answered is a subject too vast to cover in its entirety. Nevertheless, we have quoted some pertinent examples.

The Blessings of the Prophet ﷺ, and Things Being Transformed When He Touched Them

Aḥmad ibn Muhammad took permission from Abū Dharr al-Harawī, and it was narrated from al-Qāḍī Abū ʿAlī, Muhammad ibn ʿAbd al-Raḥmān, and others, from Abū al-Walīd al-Qāḍī, from Abū Dharr, from Abū Muhammad, Abū Ishāq, and Abū al-Haytham, from al-Farabrī, from Bukhārī, from ʿAbd al-Aʿlā ibn Ḥammād, from Yazīd ibn Zurayʿ, from Saʿīd, from Qatādah, from Anas ibn Mālik: "The people of Madinah were shocked to see the Prophet ﷺ riding a horse, belonging to Abū Ṭalḥah, known to have a slow, halting gait. When he returned, the Prophet ﷺ said he had found the horse to be quick and nimble, but it never broke past a canter after that."[339]

---

337 Reported by Ibn Isḥāq in *Al-Sīrah* (likewise, in the *Sīrah* of Ibn Hishām 2/628) in a *mursal* hadith narrated from al-Ḥasan al-Baṣrī.

338 The original source of the story can be found in Abū Dāwūd (3607), Nasāʾī (7/301-302), and others, from the hadith of ʿUmārah ibn Khuzaymah, who took from his uncle, who was a Companion of the Prophet ﷺ. Its chain is *ḥasan*. Also recorded by Ṭabarānī, from Khuzaymah ibn Thābit. Haythamī said in *Majmaʿ al-Zawāʾid* (9/320): "All the narrators are trustworthy."

339 The chain of the narrator is found in Bukhārī (2867). Also reported by Muslim (2307).

Once, a camel belonging to Jābir had become exhausted and worn out. When the Prophet ﷺ nudged its sides, it became so energized that he almost lost control of its reins.[340] He did something similar with a horse belonging to Ju'ayl al-Ashja'ī, patting its udder and praying for blessings. The horse became so frisky and full of vigour it could not be restrained, and went on to give birth to twelve thousand foals for trade.[341] He once rode a slow donkey belonging to Sa'd ibn 'Ubādah, and returned it as a speedy steed that no-one could keep up with.[342] Khālid ibn al-Walīd took some hairs from the donkey and kept them in his cap. Every time he wore it to battle, he was blessed with victory.[343] Asmā' bint Abī Bakr once brought out a thobe, and remembered: "The Messenger of Allah ﷺ used to wear it, and we would wash it so that people who were sick could be healed with the water."[344] Abū 'Alī reported that his teacher, Abū al-Qāsim ibn al-Ma'mūn, said: "We had a bowl belonging to the Prophet ﷺ, so we would fill it with water to heal the sick."

There was an incident where Jahjāh al-Ghifārī took the staff of the Prophet ﷺ from 'Uthmān, intending to break it across his knee. The people screamed at him not to. His knee was seized with a pain that gnawed at the joint until it had to be amputated, and he died before the year was out.[345]

---

340 Reported by Bukhārī (2718), and Muslim in *Al-Musāqāh* (715/109) from the hadith of Jābir ibn 'Abdullāh.

341 Reported by Nasā'ī with a sound chain, Bukhārī in *Al-Tārīkh*, and Bayhaqī in *Al-Dalā'il*. Also found in *Shamā'il al-Rasūl*, p. 312.

342 Related by Ibn Sa'd in *Al-Ṭabaqāt* from the hadith of Isḥāq ibn 'Abdullāh ibn Abī Ṭalḥah.

343 Reported by Abū Ya'lā (7183), Ibn al-Athīr in *Usd al-Ghāyah* (1/588), Ṭabarānī in *Al-Kabīr* (3804), and Ḥākim (3/299) from the hadith of Khālid ibn al-Walīd. Dhahabī said: "It is disconnected." Haythamī said in *Majma' al-Zawā'id* (9/349): "It was related by Ṭabarānī and Abū Ya'lā, and the narrators were sound. Ja'far heard it from several of the Companions, but I do not know if he heard it from Khālid or not." Būṣīrī said, in *Ḥāshiyat al-Muṭālib al-'Āliyah* (4044): "It was related by Abū Ya'lā with a sound chain of transmission."

344 Reported by Muslim (2069).

345 Related by Ibn al-Sakan, and others, as found in *Al-Iṣābah* (1/254-255) from the hadith of Ibn

When the Prophet ﷺ poured the leftover water after making *wuḍū'* into the well of Qubā', it never stopped flowing again.[346] He spat into a well in the home of Anas, and it became the sweetest water in all of Madinah.[347] The Prophet ﷺ once came across a source of water and asked the people about it. They told him: "It is named *Bīsān*, and is salty to taste." He replied: "Rather, it will be named *Na'mān*, and its water is pure."[348] After that, the water became sweet. He was once given a bucket of Zamzam water; he spat into it, and it became sweeter smelling than musk.[349] Another time, he gave al-Ḥasan and al-Ḥusayn his tongue to suck on; they had been crying from thirst, and they quietened down.[350] The Prophet ﷺ used to put some of his saliva onto the palate of infant children when they were sick, and it would suffice them until the night.[351]

Umm Mālik had an animal skin containing ghee which she gifted to the Prophet ﷺ. He gave it back to her and told her not to squeeze it. Her children used to come to her asking for seasoning for the food, because they did not have any. They found that the animal skin was now stuffed full of ghee, and it never ran out until she squeezed it.[352]

The hands of the Prophet ﷺ carried blessings when he planted trees for Salmān. His masters had determined the price of his freedom as three hundred trees – each one to be planted, tied, and bearing fruit – alongside

---

'Amr.

346 Related by Bayhaqī in *Al-Dalā'il* from the hadith of Anas.

347 Reported by Abū Nu'aym, also from Anas, in *Al-Manāhil,* p. 666.

348 Mentioned by Ibn Ḥajr in *Al-Iṣābah* (2/220-221).

349 Reported by Ibn Mājah (659), Aḥmad (4/315), and others, from the hadith of Wā'il ibn Ḥujr, and it does not mention "Zamzam water". Būṣīrī said in *Miṣbāḥ al-Zujājah*: "Its chain is disconnected."

350 Related by Ṭabarānī from the hadith of Abū Hurayrah. Haythamī said in *Majma' al-Zawā'id* (9/180-181): "The narrators are trustworthy."

351 Reported by Abū Ya'lā (7162).

352 Reported by Muslim (2280) from the hadith of Jābir ibn 'Abdullāh.

forty ūqiyyah[353] of gold. The Prophet ﷺ planted every tree with his own hands, bar one. All the trees took root, except for the one that somebody else had planted. The Prophet ﷺ pulled it up and re-planted it, and it took root. As al-Bazzār commented: "The trees all bore fruit from that year, except for that one. After the Messenger of Allah ﷺ had re-planted the last tree, it bore fruit from the next year on." The Prophet ﷺ gave Salmān the weight of a chicken's egg in gold after rolling it on his tongue. He weighed out the forty *ūqiyyah* to pay off his owners, and found that he still had the same amount left over.[354]

Ḥanash ibn ʿAqīl narrated: "The Messenger of Allah ﷺ gave me some *sawīq*[355] to drink. He would drink first, and I would drink after him. I found that it filled me up when I felt hungry, quenched me when I was thirsty, and cooled me down when I felt parched."[356]

Qatādah ibn al-Nuʿmān once prayed ʿishā' with the Prophet ﷺ on a dark, rainy night. The Prophet ﷺ gave him a cluster of dates and said: "Take it with you, and it will light the way in front of you and behind you. When you enter your house, you will see something dark. Strike it until it leaves, because it is the Devil (*Shayṭān*)." Qatādah left, and the cluster of dates illuminated his path. When he entered his house he did find something dark, so he beat it until it departed.[357]

When ʿUkāshah had his sword broken during the Battle of Badr, the Prophet ﷺ gave him a stick of wood and said: "Fight with this!" When

353 One *ūqiyyah* was equivalent to forty dirhams.

354 Reported by Aḥmad (5/441-444), Ṭabarānī in *Al-Kabīr* (6065), and others, from the hadith of Salmān al-Fārisī. Mentioned by Haythamī in *Majmaʿ al-Zawā'id* (9/336). See also, *Mawārid al-Ẓam'ān* (7/218).

355 A dish made from ground wheat and barley.

356 Related by Qāsim in *Al-Dalā'il*, from the narration of Mūsā ibn ʿUqbah, from al-Miswar ibn Makhramah.

357 Reported by Aḥmad (3/65) from the hadith of Abū Qatādah, and authenticated by Suyūṭī in *Al-Manāhil*, p. 674. Haythamī said in *Majmaʿ al-Zawā'id* (9/319): "The narrators in the chain of Aḥmad are reliable." Also related by Bazzār and Ṭabarānī.

ʿUkāshah looked down at his hand, he found that the wood had transformed into a sword of solid steel; tall, glistening, and razor sharp. He fought with it, and it remained with him for every battle after that, until he was martyred in the Wars of Apostasy.[358] ʿUkāshah had named the sword *al-ʿAwn*, meaning, "The Assistance". The Prophet ﷺ also helped ʿAbdullāh ibn Jaḥsh, during the Battle of Uḥud, with a branch of a date palm tree which transformed into a sword in his hand.[359]

Another miraculous blessing the Prophet ﷺ possessed was his ability to make a sheep that was no longer producing milk abundant once again. This was evidenced on several occasions, including: the story of the lamb belonging to Umm Maʿbad[360], the goat of Muʿāwiyah ibn Thawr, a lamb belonging to Anas, the sheep and the ageing female camel of Ḥalīmah[361], a lamb belonging to ʿAbdullāh ibn Masʿūd (which had never mated), and the lamb of Miqdād.

Ḥammād ibn Salamah relates an occasion when the Prophet ﷺ prepared a container of water for his Companions and recited some supplications over it. When the time for prayer arrived, they got down from their animals and went to the water. Instead, they found pure, sweet milk, topped with cream at the rim.

The Prophet ﷺ wiped over the head of ʿUmayr ibn Saʿd and prayed for blessings. When ʿUmayr passed away, at the age of eighty, he did not have a single grey hair. Similar stories were mentioned about al-Sā'ib ibn Yazīd and Madlūk. He once wiped his hand over the stomach and back of ʿUtbah ibn Farqad; the man developed a sweet scent that would over-

358 Reported by Bayhaqī in *Al-Dalā'il* from the hadith of ʿUkāshah ibn Miḥṣan.

359 Reported by Bayhaqī in *Al-Dalā'il* from Saʿīd ibn ʿAbd al-Raḥmān, who narrated it from his teachers.

360 Mentioned by Haythamī in *Majmaʿ al-Zawā'id* (8/313), from the hadith of Umm Maʿbad.

361 The wet-nurse of the Prophet ﷺ.

power the perfumes of his female relatives.[362] When ʿĀ'idh ibn ʿAmr was wounded in the Battle of Ḥunayn, the Prophet ﷺ wiped the blood from his face and prayed for him. From then on, ʿĀ'idh had a bright, striking face, like that of a stallion.[363] He also wiped the head of Qays ibn Zayd al-Judhāmī and supplicated for him. When Qays died, at the age of 100, his hair was completely white, apart from a black patch where the Prophet ﷺ had touched. He became known as "*al-Agharr*", meaning "the one with the blaze".[364] Something similar happened to ʿUmar ibn Thaʿlabah al-Juhanī.[365]

In the case of another man, said to be Khuzaymah ibn Sawād ibn al-Ḥārith, the traces of the fingertips of the Prophet ﷺ left a light emanating from his face.[366] The shine on the face of Qatādah ibn Milḥān, after the Prophet ﷺ had stroked it, was like staring into a glass mirror.[367] On another occasion, he placed his hand on the head of Ḥanẓalah ibn Ḥidhyam and made *duʿā'* for him. A man was brought to Ḥanẓalah with swelling on his face, and a lamb with a swollen udder. When each was brought into contact with the area the Prophet ﷺ had touched, their swelling subsided.[368]

After the Prophet ﷺ sprinkled some water onto the face of Zaynab

---

362 Related by Bayhaqī, and Ṭabarānī in *Al-Kabīr* and *Al-Awsaṭ*, from the hadith of ʿUtbah ibn Farqad. Haythamī said in *Majmaʿ al-Zawā'id* (8/282-283): "It was related by Ṭabarānī in *Al-Kabīr* and *Al-Awsaṭ*. The narrators in *Al-Awsaṭ* are sound, except for Umm ʿĀṣim, who is unknown to me."

363 Related by Ṭabarānī from the hadith of ʿĀ'idh ibn ʿAmr. Haythamī said in *Majmaʿ al-Zawā'id* (9/412): "It includes narrators I do not know."

364 Reported by Ibn al-Sakan, Ibn Mandah, and others. See *Al-Iṣābah* (3/237).

365 Reported by Ṭabarānī, and Bayhaqī in *Al-Dalā'il*. Haythamī said in *Majmaʿ al-Zawā'id* (9/405): "It was related by Ṭabarānī, and the narrators up until Abū Nuʿaym are trustworthy."

366 Mentioned by Suyūṭī in *Al-Manāhil*, p. 691.

367 Reported by Aḥmad (5/28-29), Bayhaqī, and Ibn Shāhīn. Haythamī said in *Majmaʿ al-Zawā'id* (9/319): "It was related by Aḥmad, and the narrators are sound."

368 Reported by Aḥmad (5/68), and Bayhaqī from the hadith of Ḥanẓalah ibn Ḥidhyam. Haythamī said in *Majmaʿ al-Zawā'id* (9/408): "It was related by Ṭabarānī in *Al-Kabīr* and *Al-Awsaṭ*, and by Aḥmad in a lengthy hadith. The narrators in the chain of Aḥmad are trustworthy."

bint Umm Salamah, she possessed a beauty not previously seen.[369] He wiped the head of a boy who had a deformity and he was healed.[370] Indeed, there were many accounts of the Prophet ﷺ touching the faces of children who had physical ailments or mental disabilities, and them subsequently recovering.

A man came to the Prophet ﷺ who had a scrotal hernia, and he was told to sprinkle it with water from a spring he had spat into. The man did so, and he was cured.[371] Ṭāwūs remembers: "Any time a person came to the Prophet ﷺ displaying signs of being possessed by a jinn or suffering from mental illness, he would rub their chest and the illness would leave them."[372]

The Prophet ﷺ once drew a bucket of water from a well, spat into it, and then poured it back inside. When he did so, the smell of musk emanated from the well. He took a fistful of dust on the day of the Battle of Ḥunayn and threw it in the direction of the disbelievers, saying: "May your faces be distorted!" The enemies were seen running and wiping filth from their eyes.[373]

Abū Hurayrah complained about being a forgetful person to the Prophet ﷺ. He was advised to spread out his garment, and he saw the Prophet ﷺ scooping something into it with his hands. He was then told to close the garment up again, and he never forgot a thing after that day.[374] There is a great deal reported about this story.

Another time, the Prophet ﷺ struck the chest of Jarīr ibn ʿAbdullāh

---

369 Related by Ṭabarānī from the hadith of Zaynab bint Umm Salamah. Haythamī said in *Majmaʿ al-Zawāʾid* (9/259): "It was related by Ṭabarānī. I do not know the narrator named Umm ʿAṭāf." Also mentioned by Ibn ʿAbd al-Barr in *Al-Istīʿāb*.

370 Related by Abū Nuʿaym from al-Wāziʿ. See *Al-Manāhil*, p. 695.

371 Mentioned by Ibn al-Athīr in *Al-Nihāyah*.

372 A *mursal* hadith. Mentioned by Suyūṭī in *Al-Manāhil*, p. 933.

373 Reported by Muslim (1777) from the hadith of Salamah ibn al-Akwaʿ.

374 Reported by Bukhārī (119), and Muslim (2492) from the hadith of Abū Hurayrah.

and supplicated for him. He had been infamous for his lack of skill in controlling and riding a horse, but he became one of the greatest horsemen of all the Arabs.[375] The Prophet ﷺ stroked the head ʿAbd al-Raḥmān ibn Zayd ibn al-Khaṭṭāb when he was still young. He was quite short, and not the most handsome child, but after the Prophet ﷺ had prayed for his blessings, he grew up to be a tall, fine young man.[376]

The Knowledge of the Prophet ﷺ Concerning Unknown and Future Events

There is an expansive wealth of hadiths concerning information the Prophet ﷺ had regarding the Unknown; they comprise a vast ocean of endless depths, and an ever-flowing fountain of knowledge. This is a subject without ambiguities, and news of this knowledge has reached us through many chains of transmission and numerous narrators, all in agreement with one another concerning the meaning and implication of that which they relate.

I was given permission to narrate the following hadith from the leading scholar, Muhammad ibn al-Walīd al-Fihrī, also known as Abū Bakr. He said: "It was narrated from Abū ʿAlī al-Tustarī, from Abū ʿUmar al-Hāshimī, from Al-Lu'lu'ī, from Abū Dāwūd, from ʿUthmān ibn Abī Shaybah, from Jarīr, from al-Aʿmash, from Abū Wā'il, from Ḥudhayfah: 'The Messenger of Allah ﷺ once addressed us, and he described every sign of the Final Hour. Whoever memorized what he said kept it with him, and whoever did not, forgot. Many friends of mine learnt this knowledge. There were some parts that I only had a vague memory of, but the details would come flooding back when I heard them mentioned, like seeing the

---

375 Reported by Bukhārī (3036), and Muslim (2475/135) from the hadith of Jarīr.

376 Mentioned by Ibn al-Athīr in *Usd al-Ghābah* (3/346). Suyūṭī attributed the narration to al-Zubayr ibn Bakkar, in *Al-Manāhil,* p. 703.

face of a person you have not met for a long time.'"[377]

Ḥudhayfah added: "I do not know if those friends of mine really forgot but, I swear by Allah, the Messenger of Allah ﷺ listed the ones who would be the leading instigators of trials and corruption at the End of Times; he mentioned three hundred people, and told us each person's name, the name of his father and the name of his tribe."[378] Abū Dharr remembered: "When the Messenger of Allah ﷺ left us, there was not a bird that flapped its wings in the sky, except he had taught us something about it."[379]

The leading scholars of hadith have recorded many instances of the Prophet ﷺ making promises to his Companions about overcoming their enemies,[380] the liberation of Makkah,[381] Yemen, Iraq, Syria,[382] and Jerusalem,[383] and the establishment of security so that a woman could travel from al-Ḥīrah (in Iraq) to Makkah, without fearing anything or anyone except Allah.[384] He predicted that Madinah would be invaded.[385]

The night before it happened, he said that ʿAlī would liberate Khaybar.[386] He told the Muslims that they would follow the divisions of the nations that had come before them[387] by splitting into seventy-three sects,

---

377 The chain of the author is from Abū Dāwūd (4240). Also reported by Bukhārī (6604) and Muslim (2891/23).

378 Reported by Abū Dāwūd (4243).

379 Reported by Aḥmad (5/153), Bazzār (147), Ṭabarānī (1647), and others. Authenticated by Ibn Ḥibbān in *Mawārid* (71), Suyūṭī in *Al-Manāhil*, p. 706. Abū Yaʿlā reports from Abū al-Dardā' with a sound chain (5109).

380 Reported by Bukhārī (3852) from the hadith of Khabbāb.

381 Reported by Bukhārī (2731, 2732) from the hadith of al-Miswar ibn Makhramah, and Marwān ibn al-Ḥakam.

382 Reported by Bukhārī (1875) and Muslim (1388) from the hadith of Sufyān ibn Abī Zuhayr.

383 Reported by Bukhārī (3176) from the hadith of ʿAwf ibn Mālik.

384 Reported by Bukhārī (3595) from the hadith of ʿAdiyy ibn Ḥātim al-Ṭā'ī.

385 Reported by Bukhārī (1874) and Muslim (1389) from the hadith of Abū Hurayrah.

386 Reported by Bukhārī (3701) and Muslim (2406) from the hadith of Sahl ibn Saʿd.

387 Reported by Bukhārī (3456) and Muslim (2669) from the hadith of Abū Saʿīd al-Khudrī.

with only one surviving with the truth,[388] all fighting over their desires and differences. He foresaw that Allah would gift his nation riches and wealth[389] like the treasures of Caesar and Khosrow.[390] They would visit each other wearing extravagant clothes, bringing out one dish after the next, and they would possess fine, patterned rugs.[391] The Prophet ﷺ said a time would come when they cover and beautify their homes as they did the Kaaba, before adding: "You are better now than you will be then."[392]

He said that the Muslims would strut arrogantly, being waited on by the women of the Romans and the Persians, and that the worst elements of society would overcome the best.[393] There would be fighting with the Turks[394], the Khazars[395] and the Romans. He promised that the Persian Empire and its leader Khosrow would fall, and the reign of the Caesars would come to an end.[396] The Roman nation, however, would continue until the end of times.[397] The Prophet ﷺ warned that, as the world drew

---

388 Reported by Aḥmad (2/332), Abū Dāwūd (4596), Tirmidhī (2640), Ibn Mājah (3991), and Abū Ya'lā (5910), from the hadith of Abū Hurayrah. Graded as authentic by Ibn Ḥibbān in *Mawārid* (1834). Also authenticated by Ḥākim (1/128), and Dhahabī concurred. Tirmidhī said: "This hadith is *ḥasan ṣaḥīḥ*." It was also related from other Companions. See the *Musnad* of Abū Ya'lā (7/32-33).

389 Reported by Bukhārī (1465) and Muslim (1052) from the hadith of Abū Sa'īd al-Khudrī.

390 Reported by Bukhārī (3121) and Muslim (2919) from the hadith of Jābir ibn Samurah. Also, Bukhārī (3120) and Muslim (2918) from the hadith of Abū Hurayrah.

391 Reported by Bukhārī (3631) and Muslim (2083) from the hadith of Jābir ibn 'Abdullāh.

392 Reported by Tirmidhī (2261) from the hadith of 'Alī. One narrator in the chain was not named. Tirmidhī said: "This hadith is *ḥasan*."

393 Reported by Tirmidhī (2261) from the hadith of Ibn 'Umar. Tirmidhī said the hadith was *gharīb*, but it was graded as *ḥasan* by Suyūṭī in *Al-Jāmi' al-Ṣaghīr* (867). Related by Ṭabarānī from Abū Hurayrah; see *Fayḍ al-Qadīr* (1/445). Haythamī said: "Its chain is *ḥasan*."

394 Reported by Bukhārī (2928) and Muslim (2912/65) from the hadith of Abū Hurayrah.

395 See Bukhārī (3590).

396 Reported by Bukhārī (3120) and Muslim (2918) from the hadith of Abū Hurayrah. Also by Bukhārī (3121) and Muslim (2919) from the hadith of Jābir ibn Samurah. See also, *Al-Jāmi' al-Ṣaghīr* (5832).

397 A *marfū'* hadith, reported by al-Ḥārith ibn Abī Usāmah, from 'Abdullāh ibn Muḥayrīz. Graded as weak by Suyūṭī in *Al-Jāmi' al-Ṣaghīr* (5832).

to a close, the most astute minds would be taken from us,[398] knowledge would diminish and great trials would proliferate, resulting in chaos and disharmony.[399] He said: "Woe to the Arabs for the evil that has come near."[400]

He stated that the authority of the Muslim nation would reach the east and the west.[401] This prophecy was fulfilled, as the Muslims have spread from the land of India to the sea of Tangier, with a force not witnessed by any nation before them. The Muslim nation has not spread in the same way towards the north or the south.

The Prophet ﷺ once said: "The people of the west (*al-gharb*) will remain upon the truth until the Final Hour is established."[402] Ibn al-Madīnī believed this to be a reference to the Arabs, because they drank from a special type of bucket also called *al-gharb*. Other scholars, however, believe the statement to refer to al-Maghrib[403].

In another hadith, transmitted by Ibn Umāmah, the Prophet ﷺ said: "A group from my nation will remain upon the truth and will be victorious over their enemies until the command of Allah arrives." The people asked: "Where will they be?" and he replied: "In Jerusalem."[404]

The Prophet ﷺ predicted the kingdom of the Umayyads[405] and the leadership of the companion Muʿāwiyah and advised him to fear Allah

398 Reported by Bukhārī (6434) from the hadith of Mirdās al-Aslamī.

399 Reported by Bukhārī (1036), and Muslim in *Al-ʿIlm* (157/11), from the hadith of Abū Hurayrah.

400 Reported by Bukhārī (3346) and Muslim (2880) from the hadith of Zaynab bint Jaḥsh.

401 Reported by Muslim (2889).

402 Reported by Muslim (1925) from the hadith of Saʿd ibn Abī Waqqāṣ.

403 Literally, "the west". Nowadays, the name is used to refer to Morocco, but historically it referred to a much larger region encompassing north and northwest Africa.

404 Haythamī said in *Majma' al-Zawā'id* (7/288): "It was related by Ṭabarānī with reliable narrators."

405 Related by Ḥākim and Tirmidhī from al-Ḥasan ibn ʿAlī; and Bayhaqī from Abū Hurayrah (see *Al-Manāhil*, p. 732).

and rule with justice.[406] He said that the Umayyads would consume the wealth of the state without spending where it was due.[407] The Prophet ﷺ also foresaw a group that would emerge from the descendants of al-ʿAbbās, carrying black flags,[408] who would take over swathes of land,[409] and he described the coming of the Mahdi[410].

The Prophet ﷺ said that his family would be persecuted and exiled and that ʿAlī specifically would be murdered.[411] He would have his beard dyed with the blood from his head at the hands of the most evil individual from his oppressors,[412] and how people treated ʿAlī would be a sign of their status in the Hereafter; his supporters would enter Paradise, and his enemies would enter the Hellfire. We now see that the ones who opposed him were the Khārijites, the Nāsibah, and a group from the Rāfiḍah who claimed to support him, but actually disbelieved in what he stood for.

---

406 Reported by Abū Yaʿlā (7380) from the hadith of Muʿāwiyah, and Aḥmad (4/101) from the hadith of Abū Umayyah ʿAmr ibn Yaḥyā ibn Saʿīd. Haythamī said in *Majmaʿ al-Zawā'id* (5/186): "It was related by Aḥmad in a *mursal* hadith, and the narrators were sound; and it was related by Abū Yaʿlā in a connected hadith, from Saʿīd, from Muʿāwiyah, and the narrators were sound; and it was related by Ṭabarānī..."

407 Reported by Abū Yaʿlā (7380) from the hadith of Abū Hurayrah, and Būṣīrī graded the chain as authentic.

408 Reported by Aḥmad, Bayhaqī, and others, from different chains of transmission. See *Al-Manāhil*, p. 735. See also, Ibn Mājah (4084).

409 Related by Ṭabarānī in *Al-Awsaṭ* from the hadith of Anas ibn Mālik. Haythamī said in *Majmaʿ al-Zawā'id* (5/187): "The chain contains Bakr ibn Yūnus, who was a weak (*ḍaʿīf*) narrator." Also related by al-ʿUqaylī in *Al-Ḍuʿafā'*. See *Al-Manāhil*, p. 736.

410 "The Divinely Guided" who will arise from the lineage of the Prophet ﷺ and rule with justice, and serve as a sign of impending trials. The story of the Mahdi has been related by the great compilers of hadith, and others, from countless chains of transmission (see *Al-Manāhil*, p. 737). These hadiths were authenticated by many leading scholars of the Sunnah. One dissenting voice was al-Ḥawt, in *Asnā al-Muṭālib*, p. 278, where he said: "All the hadiths about the Mahdi are weak." See also, *Jāmiʿ al-Uṣūl* (10/330-332), *Majmaʿ al-Zawā'id* (8/313-318), and *Al-Jāmiʿ al-Ṣaghīr* (9241-9245).

411 Reported by Ḥākim (4/487) from the hadith of al-Khudrī. He graded it as authentic, and Dhahabī concurred.

412 Related by Ṭabarānī from the hadith of ʿAlī. Haythamī said in *Majmaʿ al-Zawā'id* (5/186): "Its chain is *ḥasan*." This hadith is also narrated by ʿAmmār ibn Yāsir, Ṣuhayb al-Rūmī and Jābir ibn Samurah, as is found in *Majmaʿ al-Zawā'id* (9/136-137).

The Prophet ﷺ also warned: "'Uthmān will be killed whilst reciting from the Qur'an."[413] His killers would try to rip the clothes from his back,[414] and his blood would fall onto a specific verse of the Qur'an in front of him:[415] "God will protect you against them."[416]

The Prophet ﷺ declared that as long as 'Umar was alive, these great trials would not begin.[417] He said that al-Zubayr would declare war on 'Alī.[418] The Prophet ﷺ also predicted that the dogs of al-Ḥaw'ab would bark at one of his wives,[419] the town would be surrounded by fierce fighting and much bloodshed, and that she would only just find a way to escape.[420] This later came to pass, when 'Ā'ishah was travelling to Basra.

The Prophet ﷺ said that 'Ammār would be killed by a belligerent group.[421] They turned out to be the supporters of Mu'āwiyah. He told 'Abdullāh ibn al-Zubayr: "Woe to the people from you, and woe to you from the people!" The Prophet ﷺ said that Quzmān – who was one of the Hypocrites – would be from the people of the Hellfire,[422] even though he had been seen fighting alongside the Muslims. Quzmān eventually com-

---

413 Reported by Tirmidhī (3708) from the hadith of Ibn 'Umar. Tirmidhī said: "This hadith is *ḥasan gharīb*." See also, *Majma'* (9/89-93).

414 Reported by Tirmidhī (3705), Ibn Mājah (112) from the hadith of 'Ā'ishah. Tirmidhī said: "This hadith is *ḥasan gharīb*."

415 Reported by Ḥākim (3/103). Dhahabī said: "A pure lie."

416 *al-Baqarah*, 137.

417 Reported by Bukhārī (7096) and Muslim (144) from the hadith of Ḥudhayfah ibn al-Yamān.

418 Reported by Abū Ya'lā (666) from the hadith of 'Alī. Haythamī said in *Majma' al-Zawā'id* (7/235): "Its chain contains 'Abd al-Malik ibn Muslim. Bukhārī said: 'His hadiths are not accepted.'"

419 Reported by Aḥmad (6/52), and Abū Ya'lā (4868), and others, from the hadith of 'Ā'ishah. Authenticated by Ibn Ḥibbān in *Mawārid* (1831) and Suyūṭī. Al-Ḥaw'ab was an area close to Basra on the route from Makkah.

420 Reported by Bazzār (3273) from the hadith of Ibn 'Abbās. Haythamī said in *Majma' al-Zawā'id* (7/234): "Its narrators are trustworthy." Suyūṭī authenticated the chain in *Al-Manāhil*, p. 749.

421 Reported by Muslim (2915) from the hadith of al-Khudrī, and (2916) from Umm Salamah. See also, *Jāmi' al-Uṣūl* (9/42-45).

422 Reported by Bukhārī (2898) and Muslim (112) from the hadith of Sahl ibn Sa'd.

mitted suicide. The Prophet ﷺ once addressed Abū Hurayrah, Samurah ibn Jundub, and Ḥudhayfah, and said: "The last one of you will die in a fire."[423] They kept asking about each other. Samurah was the last to leave this life; he was old, his mind had grown weak, and he was trying to light up a fire when he fell in and was burnt to death.

He said about Ḥanẓalah al-Ghasīl (the washed one): "Ask his wife about him, because I saw the angels washing him."[424] She told them that Ḥanẓalah had gone out in a state of major impurity (*janābah*), and had not had time to bathe. Abū Sa'īd added: "When we found him, his head was dripping with water."

The Prophet ﷺ said: "The Caliphate is with the Quraysh,[425] and it will remain with them as long as they establish the religion.[426]" He also warned of a liar and a murderous tyrant, both hailing from the Thaqīf tribe.[427] Commentators have suggested that al-Mukhtār ibn Abī 'Abīd al-Thaqafī[428] was the liar, and Ḥajjāj ibn Yūsuf the tyrant. He promised that Allah Exalted would humiliate Musaylamah,[429] and cautioned about the Wars of Apostasy to come[430]. He gave Fāṭimah the good news that she would be the first from his family to reunite with him in Paradise.[431] The Prophet

---

423 Related by al-Ṭabarāni in *Al-Awsaṭ* from the hadith of Abū Hurayrah. Haythamī said in *Majma' al-Zawā'id* (7/234): "Its chain contains 'Alī ibn Zayd ibn Jud'ān; some said he was reliable, and others said he was weak. The rest of the narrators are trustworthy." Dhahabī questioned reliability of the hadith in *Al-Siyar* (3/184).

424 Related by Ibn Isḥāq from 'Āṣim ibn 'Umar ibn Qatādah, and al-Sirāj from 'Abdullāh ibn al-Zubayr. See *Al-Manāhil*, p. 754.

425 Reported by Aḥmad (4/185) from the hadith of 'Utbah ibn 'Abd al-Sulamī. Haythamī said in *Majma' al-Zawā'id* (5/196): "It was related by Aḥmad and Ṭabarānī, and the narrators of Aḥmad are reliable." Graded as *ḥasan* by Suyūṭī in *Al-Jāmi' al-Ṣaghīr*. See also, *Jāmi' al-Uṣūl* (4/42-47).

426 Reported by Bukhārī (3500) from the hadith of Mu'āwiyah ibn Abī Sufyān.

427 Reported by Muslim (2545) from the hadith of Asmā' bint Abī Bakr.

428 An extreme liar; he was killed by Muṣ'ab ibn al-Zubayr.

429 Reported by Bukhārī (3620) and Muslim (2273) from the hadith of Ibn 'Abbās.

430 See the narration of Thawbān, in Muslim (1920). See also *Jāmi' al-Uṣūl* (10/34-37).

431 Reported by Bukhārī (3626) and Muslim (2450) from the hadith of 'Ā'ishah, from Fāṭimah .

ﷺ explained that the Caliphate would last for thirty years, followed by kingdoms; that is exactly what happened, with the change beginning from the time of al-Ḥasan ibn ʿAlī. The Prophet ﷺ said: "This matter began as Prophethood and mercy, followed by mercy and a Caliphate, followed by kingdoms,[432] and, lastly, followed by tyranny, abuse and corruption amongst my people."[433]

The Prophet ﷺ knew about a devoted worshipper from Yemen named Uways al-Qarnī, who believed in him, even though they had never met.[434] Among other predictions, he said that there would be rulers of his nation that delayed the prayer beyond its time.[435] There would be thirty deceitful liars amongst the Muslims, including four women.[436] In another narration, one of these liars would be the Dajjāl, and they would all spread falsehood about Allah and His Messenger.[437]

The Prophet ﷺ made many predictions about the future state of Muslim society. He said: "Soon, there will be many non-Arabs amongst you,

---

432 Reported by Abū Dāwūd (4646), Tirmidhī (2226), Nasāʾī (see *Tuḥfat al-Ashrāf*, 4480), and others, from the hadith of Safīnah. Authenticated by Suyūṭī in *Al-Jāmiʿ al-Ṣaghīr* (4147), and Ibn Ḥibbān in *Mawārid* (1534).

433 Reported by Abū Yaʿlā (873), Bazzār (1589), and Ibn Abī ʿĀṣim in *Al-Sunnah* (1130), from the hadith of Abū ʿUbaydah and Muʿādh ibn Jabal. Haythamī said in *Majmaʿ al-Zawāʾid* (5/189): "It was related by Abū Yaʿlā and Bazzār from Abū ʿUbaydah only...and by Ṭabarānī from Muʿādh and Abū ʿUbaydah...and the chain contains Layth ibn Abī Sulaym; his narrations were reliable, but he was known to make omissions. The rest of the narrators are reliable." Haythamī mentions a similar report from Ḥudhayfah ibn al-Yamān (5/188-189): "It was related by Aḥmad in the biography of al-Nuʿmān, and Bazzār in a more complete form, and partially by Ṭabarānī in *Al-Awsaṭ*, and the narrators are trustworthy." The hadith is sound, by way of supporting narrations.

434 Reported by Muslim (2542) from the hadith of ʿUmar ibn al-Khaṭṭāb.

435 Reported by Muslim (534) from the hadith of Ibn Masʿūd.

436 Reported by Aḥmad (5/396) from the hadith of Ḥudhayfah. Haythamī said in *Majmaʿ al-Zawāʾid* (7/332): "It was related by Aḥmad, Ṭabarānī in *Al-Kabīr*, and Bazzār. The narrators of Bazzār are reliable." Suyūṭī said in *Al-Manāhil*, p. 765: "It was related by Aḥmad, Ṭabarānī, and Bazzār, with a sound chain."

437 Reported by Abū Dāwūd (4334) from the hadith of Abū Hurayrah, Bukhārī (7121), and Muslim in *Al-Fitan* (157/84) with a different wording.

who will consume your wealth and strike your necks."[438] On another occasion, he told his Companions: "The Final Hour will not be established until the people are herded by a man from Qaḥṭān."[439] He also said: "The best of you are my generation, and then the next, and the next. After that, there will be people who give testimony without being asked to do so, they trick people and cannot be trusted, they never fulfil their promises, and they go to excess in food and drink, until obesity becomes widespread."[440] The Prophet ﷺ observed: "Every epoch is followed by another containing more evil than before."[441] He warned: "My nation will be destroyed at the hands of young boys from the Quraysh." According to Abū Hurayrah, he offered to name them.[442] He knew about the Qadariyyah[443] and Rāfiḍah[444] sects, and said that later generations from his community would curse those who came before them.[445] He said that the numbers of the Anṣār would diminish, until they were like the grains of salt sprinkled onto a meal.[446] This would continue until not a single congregation of them remained. Nevertheless, the Prophet ﷺ promised that the Anṣār would

---

438 Mentioned by Haythamī in *Majma' al-Zawā'id* (7/310-311) from the hadith of Samurah, Anas, and 'Abdullāh ibn 'Amr, Ḥudhayfah, and Abū Hurayrah. Concering the latter transmission, he said: "It was related by Ṭabarānī, and the narrators are sound."

439 Reported by Bukhārī (3517) and Muslim (2910) from the hadith of Abū Hurayrah.

440 Reported by Bukhārī (2651) and Muslim (2535) from the hadith of 'Imrān ibn Ḥuṣayn.

441 Reported by Bukhārī (7068) from the hadith of Anas ibn Mālik.

442 Reported by Bukhārī (3605) from the hadith of Abū Hurayrah. See also, Muslim (2918).

443 Reported by Abū Dāwūd (4613) and Aḥmad (2/90) from the hadith of Ibn 'Umar. Authenticated by Ḥākim (1/84). Dhahabī said in *Al-Kabā'ir*: "It is authentic according to the conditions of Muslim."

444 Mentioned by Haythamī in *Majma' al-Zawā'id* (10/21-22) from the hadith of Umm Salamah, Fāṭimah, 'Alī, and Ibn 'Abbās. He said about the latter narration: "It was related by Ṭabarānī, and its chain is *ḥasan*." See also, Ibn Abī 'Āṣim in *Al-Sunnah* (pp. 460 – 462).

445 Reported by Tirmidhī (2210) from the hadith of 'Alī, and (2211) from the hadith of Abū Hurayrah; both narrations have a weak chain. Attributed in *Al-Manāhil*, p. 775 to Baghawī from 'Ā'ishah, and Ibn Mājah from Jābir.

446 Reported by Bukhārī (3800) from the hadith of Ibn 'Abbās.

leave a legacy after he was gone.[447] He also told his Companions about the reality of the Khārijites, and described their characteristics. He noted a deformed person who would be amongst them, and that they would be recognized by their shaved heads.[448]

The Prophet ﷺ spoke about strange things that would come to pass: shepherds would become leaders of the people; the barefoot, naked ones would compete in constructing tall buildings; and daughters would lord over their mothers.[449] He also foretold how battles would play out, promising that the Quraysh and their supporters would never defeat him, but he would defeat them.[450] He mentioned a devastating plague, "The Death", which would be witnessed after the liberation of Jerusalem,[451] and he related what was promised for the homes of Basra.[452] The Prophet ﷺ said that the Muslims would conquer new territories by sea, and stand in victory on the shores.[453] He said that had piety been hung in the Pleiades cluster of stars, men from Persia would have obtained it.[454]

The wind raged during one of the battles, and the Prophet ﷺ said: "It rages for the death of a Hypocrite."[455] When we got back to Madinah, we found that to be the case. During one gathering, the Prophet ﷺ told the people: "The tooth of one of you will be heavier in the Hellfire than Mount

---

447 Reported by Bukhārī (3147) and Muslim (1059) from the hadith of Anas ibn Mālik.

448 The hadith describing the characteristics of the Khārijites was reported by Bukhārī, Muslim, and others. See also, *Jāmi' al-Uṣūl* (10/86-93).

449 Reported by Bukhārī (50) and Muslim (9, 10) from the hadith of Abū Hurayrah, and Muslim (8) from the hadith of 'Umar.

450 Reported by Bukhārī (4110) from the hadith of Sulaymān ibn Ṣurd.

451 Reported by Bukhārī (3176) from the hadith of 'Awf ibn Mālik.

452 Reported by Abū Dāwūd (4307) from the hadith of Anas.

453 Reported by Bukhārī (2800) and Muslim (1912) from the hadith of Anas, from his aunt Umm Ḥarām.

454 Reported by Bukhārī (4897) and Muslim (2546) from the hadith of Abū Hurayrah.

455 Reported by Muslim (2782) from the hadith of Jābir ibn 'Abdullāh.

Uḥud."[456] Abū Hurayrah related: "Those people all passed away until just me and one other man remained. He was killed after leaving Islam, during the Battle of Yamāmah.

The Prophet ﷺ knew about the person who had stolen some decorative beads from a Jewish man. They were part of the spoils from the Battle of Khaybar that had not yet been distributed, and they were subsequently found in that person's possessions.[457] He also knew about a cloak that had been taken, and where it could be found.[458] When someone's camel had gone astray, the Prophet ﷺ told them they would find it tied to a certain tree.[459] He knew about the letter of Ḥātib ibn Abī Balta'ah,[460] who had secretly written to the disbelievers of Makkah, warning them of the Muslims' preparations to liberate the city. He was forgiven by the Prophet ﷺ, partly on account of his earlier fighting for the Muslims at the Battle of Badr. The Prophet ﷺ was also aware that Ṣafwān ibn Umayyah had persuaded 'Umayr ibn Wahb to assassinate him. When 'Umayr arrived to carry out the plot, the Prophet ﷺ informed him that he already knew about their secret. 'Umayr, amazed, immediately embraced Islam.[461] When he told the people about some money his uncle, al-'Abbās, had privately left with Umm al-Faḍl[462], his uncle said: "No-one knew about it except for me and her", and he became Muslim.[463]

---

456 Related by Ṭabarānī from the hadith of Rāfi' ibn Khadīj. Haythamī said in *Majma' al-Zawā'id* (8/290): "The chain contains al-Wāqidī, and he was a weak narrator."

457 Reported by Abū Dāwūd (2710), Nasā'ī (4/64), Ibn Mājah (2848), Mālik in *Al-Muwaṭṭa'* (2/458), and others, from the hadith of Zayd ibn Khālid al-Juhanī. Authenticated by Ḥākim (2/127), and Dhahabī concurred.

458 Reported by Bukhārī (4234) and Muslim (115) from the hadith of Abū Hurayrah.

459 Related in a *mursal* hadith by al-Bahyaqī from 'Urwah, in *Al-Manāhil*, p. 787.

460 Reported by Bukhārī (3007) and Muslim (2494) from the hadith of 'Alī.

461 Related by Ṭabarānī from the hadith of Anas ibn Mālik. Haythamī said in *Majma' al-Zawā'id* (8/287): "The narrators are sound."

462 The wife of al-'Abbās.

463 Related by Aḥmad (1/303) from the hadith of Ibn 'Abbās. Haythamī said in *Majma' al-Zawā'id*

The Prophet ﷺ correctly predicted that he would kill Ubayy ibn Khalaf, who was an evil man known for his oppression and cruelty, and he did so at the Battle of Uḥud. When ʿUtaybah – the first cousin of the Prophet ﷺ and the son of Abū Lahab – divorced his daughter Umm Kulthūm, and then physically attacked the Prophet ﷺ, he supplicated for him to be eaten by a predator from the creation of Allah. ʿUtaybah left on a trade journey to Syria, and had stopped off for the night, when a lion singled him out from the group and mauled him to death.

After the Battle of Badr, the Prophet ﷺ knew the precise location of where people had been killed.[464] He also knew who had been slain at the Battle of Mu'tah, despite being at least one month's travel away.[465] Similarly, when the Negus passed away in his own land, the Prophet ﷺ was miraculously aware of it.[466]

Speaking about al-Ḥasan, he said: "This son of mine (i.e., grandson) is a leader; perhaps Allah will use him to reconcile between two mighty factions from amongst the Muslims."[467] Of Saʿd, he said: "Perhaps you will live a long life, and you will benefit one group of people whilst another seek to cause you harm."[468]

The Prophet ﷺ informed Fayrūz al-Daylamī, a Persian man, of the death of Khosrow.[469] When, on the very same day, a messenger arrived from Persia and confirmed the news, Fayrūz became Muslim.

When the Prophet ﷺ found Abū Dharr sleeping in the mosque, he

---

(6/86): "There is one narrator who is not named, but the rest are trustworthy." Authenticated by Ḥākim (3/324) from the hadith of ʿUtbah, and Dhahabī concurred.

464 Reported by Muslim (1779) from the hadith of Anas.

465 Reported by Bukhārī (1246) from the hadith of Anas.

466 Reported by Bukhārī (1245) and Muslim (951) from the hadith of Abū Hurayrah.

467 Reported by Bukhārī (2804) from the hadith of Abū Bakr.

468 Reported by Bukhārī (4409) and Muslim (1628) from the hadith of Saʿd ibn Abī Waqqāṣ.

469 Related by Bayhaqī (see *Al-Manāhil*, p. 798).

described his impending exile: "How will it be when you are driven out of this mosque?" Abū Dharr replied that he would take residence in the Sacred Mosque instead. The Prophet ﷺ continued: "And how about when you are driven from there, too?"[470] During the Expedition to Tābūk, he told Abū Dharr that he would end up living alone, dying alone, and entering Paradise alone.[471]

He said that the first of his wives to join him in Paradise would be the most generous in spending her wealth.[472] It was Zaynab who spread her hands the furthest in charitable donations. He warned that al-Ḥusayn would be killed at al-Ṭaff[473] and as he took a handful of the earth, the Prophet ﷺ said: "His resting-place is here."[474] He said, about Zayd ibn Ṣūḥān, that one of his limbs would get to Paradise before him;[475] later, his hand was cut off in battle.

The Prophet ﷺ honoured the ones who ascended Mount Uḥud alongside him. When the mountain shook, he told it to hold firm, and said: "There is no-one upon you except a Prophet, a *siddīq*[476], and a martyr." From amongst those who accompanied him, ʿAlī, ʿUmar, ʿUthmān, Ṭalḥah and al-Zubayr were indeed martyred, and Saʿd succumbed to bat-

---

470 Related by Ṭabarānī from the hadith of Abū Dharr. Haythamī said in *Majmaʿ al-Zawāʾid* (5/223): "The narrators are trustworthy, except that Abū al-Salīl Ḍurayb ibn Nufayr did not meet Abū Dharr." A similar hadith from Asmāʾ bint Yāzīd was reported by Aḥmad (6/457), and Haythamī said in *Majmaʿ* (5/223): "Its chain includes Shahr ibn Ḥawshab, who is considered trustworthy."

471 Related by Ibn Isḥāq, with a weak chain, from Ibn Masʿūd (see *Al-Iṣābah*, 4/65). Also mentioned by Suyūṭī in *Al-Manāhil*, p. 800.

472 Reported by Bukhārī (1420) and Muslim (2452) from the hadith of ʿĀʾishah.

473 The present-day region of Karbala, in Iraq.

474 Related by Ṭabarānī in *Al-Kabīr* and *Al-Awsaṭ* from the hadith of ʿĀʾishah. Haythamī said in *Majmaʿ al-Zawāʾid* (9/187): "The chain of *Al-Kabīr* contains Ibn Lahīʿah, and the chain of *Al-Awsaṭ* contains narrators I do not know."

475 Reported by Abū Yaʿlā (511) and al-Khaṭīb in *Tārīkh Baghdād* (8/440), from the hadith of ʿAlī. Haythamī said in *Majmaʿ al-Zawāʾid* (9/398): "The chain of Abū Yaʿlā contains narrators I do not know."

476 A "truthful one", referring to Abū Bakr.

tle wounds.

The Prophet ﷺ asked Surāqah, a fearless soldier: "How will it be for you when you wear the bracelets of Khosrow?"[477] When ʿUmar later dressed him in the royal garments of Khosrow, received as part of the war spoils from the liberation of Persia, Surāqah said: "All Praise and Gratitude is for Allah, the one who took them from Khosrow and put them on me."

The Prophet ﷺ referenced Baghdad, when he said: "There will be a city constructed between the Tigris and Dujayl[478], and Quṭrabbul[479] and al-Ṣarāh[480]. The treasures of the earth will be collected there, and lost there again."[481]

He said: "There will be a man from our community named al-Walīd, and he will be even worse for us than the Pharoah was for his."[482] He also mentioned: "The Final Hour will not be established until two groups with the same calling fight each other."[483]

When the Prophet ﷺ sent Khālid ibn Walīd on an expedition to fight against Ukaydir ibn ʿAbd al-Malik, the Christian prince of Dawmat al-Jandal, he said: "You will find him hunting for wild cows."[484]

The Prophet ﷺ said to ʿUmar regarding Suhayl ibn ʿAmr: "ʿUmar!

---

477 Related by Bayhaqī in *Al-Dalā'il* (see *Al-Manāhil*, p. 805). Mentioned in a *mursal* hadith by Ibn Ḥajr, in *Al-Iṣābah* (2/18-19).

478 Literally, 'the small Tigris'. Referring to the Kārūn river in present-day Iran.

479 A settlement between Baghdad and the ancient town of ʿUkbarā.

480 A river inside Baghdad.

481 Related by al-Khaṭīb in Al-Tārīkh, and Abū Nuʿaym in Al-Dalā'il, from Jarīr ibn ʿAbdullāh (see *Al-Manāhil*, p. 806).

482 Reported by Aḥmad (1/18) from the hadith of ʿUmar, and declared as *ḥasan* by Bayhaqī (see *Al-Manāhil*, p. 807; and *Majmaʿ al-Zawā'id*, 5/240). Ibn Ḥibbān said in *Al-Majrūḥīn*: "This is a false report." Ibn al-Jawziyy concurred with Ibn Ḥibbān. The hadith was also reported by Maʿmar ibn Rāshid in *Al-Jāmi*ʿ (19861).

483 Reported by Bukhārī (3608) and Muslim in *Al-Fitan* (157/17).

484 A *mursal* hadith, reported by Ibn Isḥāq and Bayhaqī, from Yazīd ibn Rūmān and ʿAbdullāh ibn Abī Bakr. Ibn Mandah connected the chain. Also reported by Abū Nuʿaym.

Perhaps, one day, he will be in a position to cheer you up."[485] When the Companions heard of the passing of the Prophet ﷺ, Suhayl stood strong like Abū Bakr did: speaking to the people, making them firm, and deepening their sense of perspective.

All the events we have mentioned came to pass just as the Prophet ﷺ predicted, either during his life, or after his passing from this life.

Not only was he aware of the Companions' innermost thoughts and secrets, but he would also tell them about the Hypocrites' disbelief, which was only displayed in private, and what they were discussing behind closed doors. It reached a point where one of the Hypocrites would say to another: "Be quiet! I swear by Allah, if he [the Prophet ﷺ] does not have a person informing him, then the stones on the ground would inform him!"

He knew the type of magic that Labīd ibn al-Aʿṣam had used against him. The magic was discovered as the Prophet ﷺ had described: tied in a comb with stray hairs, discarded into the well of Dharwān, in the pollen-producing stamens of a male date palm.

The Prophet ﷺ told the Quraysh that termites would devour the documents they had used to cut off ties with the Banū Hāshim clan, except that every mention of the name of Allah would remain unscathed.[486] When the papers were found, it proved to be true. He also gave the disbelievers of Quraysh a precise description of Jerusalem, after they doubted the authenticity of his miraculous Night Journey, with a level of detail that only someone who had truly seen the city would be able to provide. Not only that, but he alerted them to a trade caravan he had passed on the way back, and told them the exact time it would arrive.[487]

The Prophet ﷺ once said: "The prosperity of Jerusalem will be the

---

485 Reported by Ḥākim (3/282), and Bayhaqī in *Al-Dalā'il*; a *mursal* hadith from the chain of al-Ḥasan ibn Muhammad.

486 Recorded by Ibn Kathīr in *Al-Sīrah* (2/45) in a *mursal* hadith, from al-Zuhrī.

487 Mentioned by Haythamī in *Majma'* (1/74) from the hadith of Shadād ibn Aws.

ruin of Yathrib[488], the ruin of Yathrib will lead to intense conflict, and this intense conflict will culminate in the liberation of Constantinople."[489]

He was able to inform the Companions of the preconditions of the Last Hour, the signs of its arrivals, the manner in which people would be resurrected and gathered and the situation of those who were righteous and those who were committed to evil. He described Paradise and the Hellfire, and the horrors and tribulations people would witness on the Final Day.

An entire volume could be dedicated to this section alone, but we will suffice with what we have mentioned.

Allah Protecting the Prophet ﷺ from the People

Allah Exalted says: "And Allah will certainly protect you from the people."[490] "So be patient with your Lord's decree, for you are truly under Our watchful Eyes."[491] He also asks: "Is Allah not sufficient for His servant?"[492] The verse was said to mean, enough for our Master Muhammad ﷺ against his enemies from the idol-worshippers, although there are also other interpretations. Allah Exalted confirms: "Surely We will be sufficient for you against the mockers."[493]

He mentions: "And remember, O Prophet, when the disbelievers conspired to capture, kill, or exile you. They planned, but Allah also planned. And Allah is the best of planners."[494]

I read the following hadith to the esteemed scholars Abū ʿAlī al-Ṣadafī

---

488 Another name for Madinah.

489 Known today as Istanbul, in Turkey. Reported by Abū Dāwūd (4294) and Aḥmad (5/232) from Muʿādh ibn Jabal.

490 *al-Mā'idah*, 67.

491 *al-Ṭūr*, 48.

492 *al-Zumar*, 36

493 *al-Ḥijr*, 95

494 *al-Anfāl*, 30.

and Muhammad ibn ʿAbdullāh al-Maʿāfirī, who both said that it was narrated from Abū al-Ḥusayn al-Ṣayrafī, from Abū Yaʿlā al-Baghdādī, from Abū ʿAlī al-Sinjī, from Abū al-ʿAbbās al-Marwaziyy, from Abū ʿĪsā al-Ḥāfiẓ, from ʿAbd ibn Ḥumayd, from Muslim ibn Ibrāhīm, from Al-Ḥārith ibn ʿUbayd, from Saʿīd al-Jurayrī, from ʿAbdullāh ibn Shaqīq, from ʿĀ'ishah, who said: "The Prophet ﷺ had people guarding him, until the verse was revealed: "Allah will certainly protect you from the people."[495] After that, the Messenger of Allah ﷺ leaned outside and called: "My people! You can depart, because I have received protection from my Lord, the Almighty."[496]

On one occasion, the Prophet ﷺ had stopped off on a journey, and the Companions chose a tree for him to take a nap under. A Bedouin man came to him, brandishing his sword, and said: "Who will protect you from me?" The Prophet ﷺ replied: "Allah." The Bedouin's hand trembled violently and he dropped the sword, and he struck his head on the tree so hard that it streamed profusely. Then, the above verse was revealed.[497] The man in the story was named Ghawrath ibn al-Ḥārith, and he reported that the Prophet ﷺ subsequently forgave him. So, he returned to his people, saying: "I was with the best of mankind."[498] An event like this also happened during the Battle of Badr. The Prophet ﷺ left his Companions to go and relieve himself, and he was pursued by one of the Hypocrites, when something similar occurred.[499]

Another hadith clarifies that the incident involving Ghawrath, also

---

495 *al-Mā'idah*, 67.

496 The chain of the author is from Tirmidhī (3046); authenticated by Ḥākim (2/313) and Dhahabī concurred.

497 Reported by Jarīr, from the hadith of Muhammad ibn Kaʿb al-Qurṭī. A *mursal* hadith.

498 Reported by Ibrāhīm al-Ḥarbī in *Gharīb al-Hadīth*, from Jābir ibn ʿAbdullāh. Reported in another context by Bukhārī (4135, 4136) and Muslim (843).

499 Mentioned by Suyūṭī in *Al-Manāhil*, p. 816.

known Du'thūr ibn al-Ḥārith, took place during the expedition that confronted the Ghaṭafān tribe at Dhāt al-Riqā'. He was known for being brave, and a leader, so when he returned to his people, who had encouraged him in his intentions to assassinate the Prophet ﷺ, they asked: "What happened regarding that which you said you would carry out if you had the opportunity?" He replied: "I saw a tall, bright figure, who pushed me in the chest. I fell onto my back and dropped the sword from my hand. I realized that it was an angel, so I accepted Islam."[500] According to the narration of al-Khaṭṭābī, Ghawrath intended to kill the Prophet ﷺ, who only became aware of the plot when he found Ghawrath standing next to his head with his sword raised. The Prophet ﷺ said: "Allah! Deal with him however you wish!" Ghawrath felt a searing pain between his shoulder blades and fell onto his face, and his sword fell from his hand. The commentators said that the following verse was revealed concerning this event: "O believers! Remember Allah's favour upon you: when a people sought to harm you, but He held their hands back from you. Be mindful of Allah. And in Allah let the believers put their trust."[501] It was said that the Prophet ﷺ had been afraid of the Quraysh, but when this verse was revealed, he lay down, and said: "Whoever wants to harm me will be left disappointed."[502]

'Abd ibn Ḥumayd mentioned that the wife of Abū Lahab – described in the Qur'an as "the carrier of thorny kindling"[503] – would place burning coals in the path of the Messenger of Allah ﷺ, but it would be as if he was walking on soft sand.[504] Ibn Isḥāq said that when she heard about the revelation of Surah al-Masad, and the way she and her husband had

---

500 Reported by al-Wāqidī in *Al-Maghāzī* (1/194-196) from 'Abdullāh ibn Abī Bakr and others. A *mursal* hadith.

501 *al-Mā'idah*, 11.

502 Related by Ibn Jarīr from Ibn Jurayj.

503 *al-Masad*, 4.

504 A *mursal* hadith, related Ibn Jarīr in his *Tafsīr*.

been cursed, she went to where the Messenger of Allah ﷺ was sitting with Abū Bakr in the mosque, carrying a stone pestle in her hand. When she stopped in front of them, she could only see Abū Bakr, as Allah had prevented her from viewing the Prophet ﷺ. She cried: "Abū Bakr! Where is your friend? I have heard that he has been mocking me. I swear by Allah, if I had found him here, I would have smashed his mouth with this pestle."[505]

Al-Ḥakam ibn Abī al-ʿĀṣ related: "We conspired and plotted to attack the Prophet ﷺ, but when we saw him, we heard a sound behind us so terrible and piercing that we thought no-one in Tihāmah would survive. We were rendered unconscious. When we came to, he had already completed his prayer and returned to his family. We tried again another night, but the mountains of Ṣafā and Marwah came and blocked us from reaching him."[506]

ʿUmar reported: "Myself and Abū Jahm ibn Ḥudhayfah agreed that we would kill the Messenger of Allah ﷺ one night, and went to his house to carry out the plan. As we listened out for him, we heard him recite: "The Inevitable Hour! What is the Inevitable Hour? And what will make you realize what the Inevitable Hour is? Both Thamūd and ʿĀd denied the Striking Disaster. As for Thamūd, they were destroyed by an overwhelming blast. And as for ʿĀd, they were destroyed by a furious, bitter wind which Allah unleashed on them non-stop for seven nights and eight days, so that you would have seen its people lying dead like trunks of uprooted palm trees. Do you see any of them left alive?"[507] Abū Jahm struck ʿUmar on the upper arm and said "Save yourself!", and they both fled the scene.

---

505 Reported by Abū Yaʿlā (53), al-Ḥumaydī (325), and others, from Asmā' bint Abī Bakr. Authenticated by Ḥākim (2/361), and Dhahabī concurred.

506 Related by Ṭabarānī and Abū Nuʿaym, with a good chain. Haythamī said in *Majmaʿ al-Zawā'id* (8/227): "The narrators are reliable, except for Bint al-Ḥakam, who I do not know."

507 *al-Ḥāqqah*, 1-8.

This was the beginning of ʿUmar's journey to Islam.[508]

There is another famous example where the Prophet ﷺ feared for his life. The Quraysh had besieged him in his home, having resolved to murder him, and lay in wait all night. He came out of his house and stood right in front of them, but Allah had blurred their vision and blinded the Quraysh.[509]

He was protected from being seen when he was in the cave with Abū Bakr, fleeing attempts on his life in Makkah, by the miraculous signs Allah had prepared for him. There was the spider which spun its web across the mouth of the cave, so that when his pursuers went to enter, Umayyah ibn Khalaf said: "How can there be anyone in this cave? This spider's web has probably been here since before Muhammad was born!" Another of the Quraysh noticed two doves stationed at the entrance of the cave, and said: "If there was anyone inside, these doves would not have stopped here."

Whilst the Prophet ﷺ and Abū Bakr were migrating to Madinah, Surāqah ibn Mālik ibn Juʿshum heard that the Quraysh had placed a bounty on their heads, so he followed them on horse. When he got close, the Prophet ﷺ began to supplicate against him, and his horse's feet sunk into the ground, throwing him off its back. He decided to consult his "divining arrows" to help choose his next course of action, and he did not like what he saw. Again he caught up with them, until he came close enough to hear the Prophet ﷺ reciting. The Prophet ﷺ did not turn around, but Abū Bakr did, and he told him that Surāqah was catching up. The Prophet ﷺ replied: "Do not fear, because Allah is with us." Surāqah's horse sunk into the ground for a second time, this time up to its knees, and again he

---

508 Reported by Aḥmad (1/17) from Shurayḥ ibn ʿAbīd, from ʿUmar. Haythamī said in *Majmaʿ al-Zawāʾid* (9/62): "The narrators are reliable, except Shurayḥ ibn ʿAbīd did not meet ʿUmar."

509 Related by Ibn Isḥāq and Bayhaqī. Reported by Ibn Mardawayh with a weak chain from Ibn ʿAbbās. A similar hadith is mentioned by Haythamī in *Majmaʿ al-Zawāʾid* (8/228), and he said: "Aḥmad related it from two chains of transmission; the narrators of one of the chains were reliable."

was thrown off. He scolded his horse and when it got back up from the ground, it appeared as if smoke was emanating from its feet.

Surāqah called out, requesting a safe passage, and the Prophet ﷺ granted it to him. It was either Abū Bakr or his freed slave, ʿĀmir ibn Fuhayrah, who wrote out the agreement. He told them about the reward the Quraysh were offering, so the Prophet ﷺ commanded him not to allow anyone to pursue them. Some narrators add that Surāqah said to the Prophet ﷺ and Abū Bakr: "I saw you supplicating against me, so now supplicate in my favour." They did so, and he was saved from punishment. When he went back to the people, Surāqah did his best to conceal the route of the Prophet ﷺ, telling them: "I have already looked; he is not there."[510] Another narration says that a shepherd had seen the Prophet ﷺ and Abū Bakr, and set off to inform the Quraysh. However, when he got back to Makkah, he was made to forget his intention, and had no recollection of what had occurred.

Ibn Isḥāq and others mentioned an incident when Abū Jahl arrived, holding a rock, while the Prophet ﷺ was prostrating in prayer. As the Quraysh watched on, he set himself to smash the rock onto the head of the Prophet ﷺ. Suddenly, his hands seized up and stuck to his neck, and he retreated on his heels. They had to ask the Prophet ﷺ to supplicate for his hands to be freed. When the Quraysh asked Abū Jahl why he had retreated after promising them to carry out a brutal assault, he said that he had been confronted with a powerful bull camel, the likes of which he had never seen before, that he feared was about to eat him. The Prophet ﷺ said: "That was Jibrīl, and if Abū Jahl came any closer he would have seized him."[511] Similarly, al-Samarqandī remembers when a man from the

---

510 The story of Surāqah is related by Bukhārī (3906) from Surāqah himself; by Bukhārī (3908) and Muslim in *Al-Zuhd* (2009/75) from al-Barāʾ ibn ʿĀzib; and by Bukhārī (3911) from Anas.

511 Mentioned by Ibn Kathīr in *Al-Sīrah* (1/464-465) from Muhammad ibn Isḥāq. Also, reported by Bukhārī (4958) from Anas.

Banū al-Mughīrah tribe came to the Prophet ﷺ, intending to kill him. Allah miraculously prevented the man from seeing the Prophet ﷺ by casting a veil over his sight, although he could hear his speech. When he went back to his people, he could not see them either, until they called out to him. Allah revealed in response:[512] "It is as if We have put shackles around their necks up to their chins so their heads are forced up, and have placed a barrier before them and a barrier behind them and covered them all up, so they fail to see the truth."[513]

Ibn Isḥāq and others also describe when the Prophet ﷺ went out to the tribe of Banū Qurayẓah, and was sitting with his back against the wall of one of their fortresses. A man from the tribe named ʿAmr ibn Jiḥāsh sent someone to drop a pair of heavy millstones (used for grinding grains) onto the Prophet ﷺ, but he stood up before they had the opportunity. He rushed back to Madinah and informed the people of what had happened.[514] According to some commentators, it was then that Allah revealed: "O believers! Remember Allah's favour upon you: when a people sought to harm you, but He held their hands back from you. Be mindful of Allah. And in Allah let the believers put their trust."[515]

As al-Samarqandī narrates, the Prophet ﷺ had an encounter with another Jewish tribe, the Banū Naḍīr, seeking compensation for the two men from the Banū Kalb tribe who had been killed by ʿAmr ibn Umayyah. Ḥuyayy ibn Akhṭab said: "Rest Abū al-Qāsim and let us feed you and provide what you have asked for." So, the Prophet ﷺ sat down, alongside Abū Bakr and ʿUmar – all the while Huyayy had secretly agreed with the Banū Naḍīr that he would assassinate him. Jibrīl came and informed the Proph-

---

512 Related by Abū Nuʿaym in *Al-Dalā'il*, from Ibn ʿAbbās.

513 *Yāsīn*, 8-9.

514 Reported by Ibn Isḥāq from the hadith of Yazīd ibn Rūmān (see Ibn Kathīr, *Al-Sīrah*, 3/162). Suyūṭī attributes it to al-Kalbī in *Al-Manāhil*, p. 827.

515 *al-Mā'idah*, 11.

et ﷺ of the plot, so he got up and pretended to need to relieve himself; instead, he hastily made his way back to Madinah.[516]

Abū Hurayrah said: Abū Jahl once promised that if he saw the Prophet ﷺ praying, he would stamp on his neck. So, when the people saw the Prophet ﷺ busy in prayer, they informed Abū Jahl. As he came near, he suddenly turned on his heels and fled, shielding himself with his hands. The people asked what had happened. Abū Jahl replied that as he approached, he had seen a trench beneath him containing a raging fire which almost consumed him. He added: "I witnessed an overwhelming scene, and heard a pounding of wings which filled the earth." The Prophet ﷺ said: "Those were angels, and if he had come any closer, they would have torn him limb from limb."[517] Then, Allah revealed to his Messenger ﷺ: "Most certainly, one exceeds all bounds once they think they are self-sufficient. But surely to your Lord is the return of all. Have you seen the man who prevents a servant of Ours from praying? What if this servant is rightly guided, or encourages righteousness? What if that man persists in denial and turns away? Does he know that Allah sees all? But no! If he does not desist, We will certainly drag him by the forelock – a lying, sinful forelock. So let him call his associates. We will call the wardens of Hell. Again, no! Never obey him O Prophet! Rather, continue to prostrate and draw near to Allah."[518]

Shaybah ibn ʿUthmān al-Ḥajabī, whose father and uncle had been killed by Ḥamzah, saw the Prophet ﷺ at the Battle of Ḥunayn. He said: "Today, I will take my revenge on Muhammad." During the melee, he crept up behind the Prophet ﷺ and raised his sword to strike. Shaybah remembered: "As I got close to him, there were huge, smokeless flames

---

516 Related by Bayhaqī from ʿUrwah (see *Al-Manāhil*, p. 828). A *mursal* hadith.

517 Reported by Muslim (2898).

518 *al-ʿAlaq*, 6-19.

soaring in front of me faster than lightning, so I turned to flee. The Prophet ﷺ perceived my presence and called me over to him, and placed his hand on my chest. He had been the person I hated the most, but when he lifted his hand again, the Prophet ﷺ had become, to me, the most beloved of all creation. He called me to fight in the path of Allah, so I protected him with my sword and my body. If I had met my father at that moment, I would have set on him rather than see the Prophet ﷺ harmed.[519]

Faḍālah ibn ʿUmayr reported: "I had a plan to assassinate the Prophet ﷺ, during the year that Makkah was liberated. He was circumambulating the Kaaba and I approached. The Prophet ﷺ called me, and asked: 'What were you whispering to yourself?' I said: 'Nothing.' He laughed, prayed for forgiveness for me, and placed his hand on my chest." Faḍālah commented: "My heart became tranquil. I swear by Allah, by the time he lifted his hand, there was not one person or thing more beloved to me than Prophet ﷺ."[520]

There is also the famous story of ʿĀmir ibn al-Ṭufayl and Arbad ibn Qays; when they came to the Prophet ﷺ, ʿĀmir said to Arbad: "I will distract Muhammad so that you can attack him." When he saw that Arbad had not taken action, he questioned him. Arbad replied: "Every time I went to strike, you were between myself and Muhammad, so how could I?"[521]

Many of the Jews and the Christian priests warned the Quraysh about the way the Prophet ﷺ always overcame their plots and schemes, and tried to persuade and cajole them into killing him. But, as the Prophet ﷺ himself observed, in the hadith of Jābir ibn ʿAbdullāh, Allah would strike

519 Mentioned by Suyūṭī in *Al-Manāhil*, p. 830, and Ibn Ḥajr in *Al-Iṣābah* (2/157).

520 Ibn Ḥajar points towards the chain of the author in *Al-Iṣābah*. Suyūṭī attributes it to Ibn Isḥāq in *Al-Manāhil*, p. 831.

521 Related by Bayhaqī and Ibn Isḥāq without a chain. Abū Nuʿaym recorded it with a chain from ʿUrwah in *Al-Dalā'il* (see *Al-Manāhil*, p. 832). A *mursal* hadith.

fear into heart of his enemies, even if they were one month's journey away, in order to give him victory.[522] This too was part of the protection of Allah; He preserved His Messenger ﷺ until his mission was complete.

The Knowledge of the Prophet ﷺ

The mesmerizing miracles of the Prophet ﷺ also encompassed the knowledge and understanding of multiple sciences that Allah bestowed upon him. He was an expert both in matters of the religion, and of the worldly life. He was well-versed in the legal principles of other religions, and he knew about the politics and interests of his community. He knew the stories of previous Prophets, mighty leaders, tyrants, and communities, and how long they lived for, all the way from Adam up to his own generation, and he was well-acquainted with their books and laws. The Prophet ﷺ knew about their hardships and battles, the descriptions of their notables, and their differences of opinion. Because of this, he could discuss with every community that rejected Islam, including the People of the Book, by using what was contained in their own scriptures. He would judge between them according to their own laws, inform them of the secret knowledge of their sciences, and uncover that which they concealed and altered.

The Prophet ﷺ knew the different Arab dialects, and the rare usage of words by certain tribes. He had mastered the eloquence of the pure language of the Arabs; he understood their wisdoms and metaphors, and the meaning of their poetry. This mastery of the language allowed him to compose maxims and examples that would strengthen the understanding of the people, ease their difficulties, and clarify obscure matters. The Shariah was neither lax nor contradictory, and it included good character,

---

522 Reported by Bukhārī (335) and Muslim (521).

excellent manners, and every desirable character trait. Not even an atheist of sound intellect could argue with what it contained, except the most uncompromising from amongst them. Every person who had opposed or rejected the Prophet ﷺ during the times of ignorance, and then heard what he was calling them to, confirmed that it was an excellent way to conduct affairs, and did not try to prove him wrong. He made pure things lawful for them, and filthy things were forbidden. He protected their lives, wealth and property from punishments in this life, and made them fear the Fire of the Hereafter.

Even to encompass some of the knowledge the Prophet ﷺ possessed would require a preoccupation with study and dedication to the books of any particular subject. The fields in which he was fluent included medicine, the interpretation of dreams, the laws of inheritance, mathematics, genealogy, and other sciences in which he is taken as an authority.

Many of the statements the Prophet ﷺ made shed a light on his knowledge. He once said that dreams should only be interpreted by those who truly understand them[523], because they hover above a person and fall with the meaning they are given[524]. He also mentioned: "Dreams consist of three types: a true dream, a dream stemming from a person's inner conversation with themselves, and nightmares from Shayṭān."[525] He added: "A time is near when even the dreams of a believer will come close to deceit."[526]

He said: "The root of every illness is indigestion."[527] In the hadith of

---

523 Reported by Ibn Mājah (3915) from Anas. Būṣīrī said in *Al-Zawā'id*: "The chain includes Yazīd ibn Abān al-Raqāshī, and he is a weak narrator."

524 Reported by Abū Dāwūd (5020), Tirmidhī (2278), Ibn Mājah (3914), and others. Authenticated by Ibn Hibbān in *Mawārid* (1795). Also graded as authentic by Ḥākim (4/390), and Dhahabī concurred.

525 Reported by Muslim (2263) from Abū Hurayrah. See also, Bukhārī (7017).

526 Reported by Bukhārī (7017) and Muslim (2263) from Abū Hurayrah.

527 Suyūṭī said in *Al-Durr al-Manthūr* that Dāraquṭnī had considered it weak.

Abū Hurayrah, the Prophet ﷺ observed: "The stomach is the basin of the body, and the veins reach it."[528] He mentioned the best types of medicine for ailments affecting the ears and the sides of the mouth, and how to use cupping (*ḥijāmah*) and laxatives.[529] He gave the best days for *ḥijāmah* as the seventeen, nineteenth, and twenty-first of each month.[530] He also spoke about seven healing properties of agarwood.[531] The Prophet ﷺ said: "The son of Adam has not filled any container worse than his stomach. If he must, then let him leave one-third for food, one-third for drink, and one-third to breathe."

When he was asked if Saba' was the name of a man, a woman, or a land, he answered: "He was a man who had ten children; six in Yemen, and four in Syria."[532] The Arabs had a strong interest in matters of genealogy, and the Prophet ﷺ responded to their questions about the lineage of Quḍā',[533] and others that they disagreed about amongst themselves. On one occasion, he said: "Ḥimyar is the head of the Arabs, Madhḥij is their crown and honour, al-Azd is the backbone of the people, and Hamdān is the pinnacle of excellence."[534]

The Prophet ﷺ said during the Farewell Pilgrimage: "The divisions of

---

528 Related by Ṭabarānī in *Al-Awsaṭ*. Haythamī said in *Majma'*: "The chain includes Yaḥyā ibn 'Abdullāh al-Bābalatī, and he is a weak narrator."

529 Reported by Tirmidhī (2047, 2048, 2053) from Ibn 'Abbās. Tirmidhī said: "The hadith is *ḥasan gharīb*."

530 Reported by Tirmidhī (2053) from Ibn 'Abbās. Authenticated by Ḥākim (4/210), and Dhahabī concurred. Tirmidhī said: "The hadith is *ḥasan gharīb*." See also, *Jāmi' al-Uṣūl* (7/542-544).

531 Reported by Bukhārī (5713) and Muslim (2214) from Umm Qays bint Miḥṣan.

532 Reported by Tirmidhī (3222), Abū Dāwūd (3988), and Ḥākim (2/424). Tirmidhī said: "The hadith is *ḥasan gharīb*." Authenticated by Ḥākim (2/423), and Dhahabī concurred. Haythamī said in *Majma' al-Zawā'id* (1/193, 7/94): "It was related by Aḥmad and Ṭabarānī. The chain contains Ibn Lahī'ah, who was weak. The rest of the narrators are reliable."

533 Reported by Aḥmad, Abū Ya'lā (1567), Bazzār, and Ṭabarānī. Haythamī said: "The chain contains Ibn Lahī'ah."

534 Reported by Bazzār (3/305, no. 2807) from 'Uthman. Haythamī graded the hadith as *ḥasan*, in *Majma'*. Ibn Ḥajr said it was *munkar*.

time (i.e., the twelve months of the year) have returned to their original form, as they were when Allah created the heavens and the earth."[535]

He described the Basin of Paradise (*al-Ḥawḍ*) as having corners of equal size. Regarding the remembrance of Allah, he said: "The good deed is rewarded with ten like it, so 150 [words of remembrance] on the tongue, are equal to 1,500 [good deeds] on the scales."[536]

The Prophet ﷺ was at a certain place when he said: "This would be the best location for a public bath (*ḥamm*ām)."[537] Another time, he said: "Everything between the east and the west is a *qiblah*."[538] He told one of the Companions – some say it was ʿUyaynah ibn Ḥiṣn al-Fazārī, others say al-Aqraʿ ibn Ḥābis al-Tamīmī – that he was more knowledgeable than them about horses.[539]

The Prophet ﷺ once told a scribe: "Keep your pen behind your ear, so it will be easier to remember where it is."[540] Despite the fact that he is described as *ummi*, he still had knowledge about such matters, even giving instructions on how certain letters should be calligraphed. As Ibn Shaʿbān[541] related, from the narration of Ibn ʿAbbās, he told people not to lengthen individual letters when writing "*bismillāh al-Raḥmān al-*

---

535 Reported by Bukhārī (3197) and Muslim (1679) from Abū Bakr.

536 Reported by Abū Dāwūd (5065), Tirmidhī (3410), Nasā'ī (3/74), and Ibn Mājah (926), from the hadith of ʿAbdullāh ibn ʿAmr ibn al-ʿĀṣ. Authenticated by Nawawī in *Al-Adhkār* (no. 204), and Ibn Ḥajr. Tirmidhī said: "The hadith is *ḥasan ṣaḥīḥ*."

537 Related by Ṭabarānī in *Al-Kabīr* from Abū Rāfiʿ. Haythamī said in *Majmaʿ al-Zawā'id* (1/279): "The chain contains Yaḥyā ibn Yaʿlā, who was weak."

538 Reported by Tirmidhī (344) and Ibn Mājah (1011). Bukhārī confirms the strength of the hadith in *Bulūgh al-Marām* (208). Tirmidhī said: "The hadith is *ḥasan ṣaḥīḥ*."

539 Reported by Aḥmad (4/387) from ʿAmr ibn ʿAbasah. Haythamī said in *Majmaʿ al-Zawā'id* (10/43): "Aḥmad reported it with a connected chain and a *mursal* chain…and the narrators are trustworthy."

540 Reported by Tirmidhī (2714), and Ibn Ḥibbān in *Al-Majrūḥīn* (2/180) from the hadith of Zayd ibn Thābit. Tirmidhī, and Suyūṭī in *Al-Jāmiʿ al-Ṣaghīr*, both graded the chain as weak.

541 He was Muhammad ibn al-Qāsim ibn Shaʿbān al-ʿAmmārī, one of the children of ʿAmmār ibn Yāsir. Dhahabī said he was a person of the Sunnah, and he died in 355 AH. His biography can be found in *Siyar A'lām al-Nubalā'* (16/78-79).

Raḥīm".[542] In another hadith, Muʿāwiyah said that he was once writing in front of the Prophet ﷺ when he said to him: "Keep the ink neatly in its stand, establish the letter *bā'*, and distinguish the letter *sīn*, and do not neglect the letter *mīm*. Beautify your writing of the name of Allah, lengthen 'al-Raḥmān', and embellish 'al-Raḥīm'."[543] It is not unlikely that although the Prophet ﷺ was himself *ummi*, Allah had blessed him with the knowledge to guide others in the pursuit. As for his knowledge of the various dialects of the Arabs, and his understanding of their poetry, this is a well-known fact that has been documented and established.

On top of that, the Prophet ﷺ was blessed with knowledge of other languages. He used to say "*sannah, sannah*",[544] which meant "good" in one of the languages of Ethiopia. He also referred to an increase in "*harj*", meaning "killing". In a narration from Abū Hurayrah, the Prophet ﷺ is quoted as asking about "*ashkanb dardam*"[545] which was Persian for "stomach ache". Speaking a number of languages would usually require a lifetime of dedicated and persistent study. But here was a man – described as *ummi* – who could. The Prophet ﷺ had not been taught by his Companions, or by the people he grew up with, and he was not known for any specialism in the subject. As Allah Exalted says: "You, O Prophet, could not read any writing even before this revelation, nor could you write at all. Otherwise, the people of falsehood would have been suspicious."[546]

The Arabs' favourite sciences were genealogy, poetry, and rhetoric. They excelled in these fields through thorough investigation, and patient, dedicated study. Despite this, what they had was nothing more than a

---

542 Suyūṭī said, in *Al-Manāhil*: "I did not come across this narration." He also said, in *Nasīm al-Riyāḍ*: "Ibn Ḥazm said it was weak."

543 Related by al-Daylamī in *Musnad al-Firdaws*.

544 Reported by Bukhārī (3874) from Umm Khālid bint Khālid.

545 Reported by Ibn Mājah (3458).

546 *al-ʿ*Ankabūt, 48.

drop in the ocean when compared to the knowledge of the Prophet ﷺ.

Even an atheist will not find a way to argue with what we have presented. The disbelievers have no trick or ruse convincing enough to disprove our evidence, and instead they resort to baseless accusations against the Qur'an and the Prophet ﷺ, such as "ancient fables"[547] and "No one is teaching him except a human."[548] Allah Exalted rebuffs their claims: "But the man they refer to speaks a foreign tongue whereas this Qur'an is in eloquent Arabic."[549]

Other notable figures tried to claim that the Prophet ﷺ had been taught either by Salmān the Persian, or by a Greek slave. As for Salmān, he did not meet the Prophet ﷺ until after the migration to Madinah, when much of the Qur'an had already been revealed. As for the Greek slave, he became a Muslim and used to study under the Prophet ﷺ. There is some disagreement about his name, with Bal'ām, Ya'īsh, Jabr and Yasār all given as possibilities. Others say he used to sit with the Prophet ﷺ at Marwah[550]. Both Salmān and the Greek spoke foreign languages, and they were undoubtedly eloquent and proficient in their own tongues. But if the Quraysh, who were fluent in Arabic, were incapable of imitating the Qur'an, or even producing one surah like it in beauty or composition, then how would non-Arabs be able to do so? The two of them remained with the Prophet ﷺ and conversed with them throughout their lives; so, have they been recorded as saying anything that resembles the revelation Prophet Muhammad ﷺ arrived with? If Salmān or the Greek had taught the Prophet ﷺ, then what would have prevented his enemies – with their greatness in number, the persistence of their efforts, and the strength of their envy – from sitting with them and learning the same? Naḍr ibn

547 *al-An'ām*, 25.

548 *al-Naḥl*, 103.

549 *al-Naḥl*, 103.

550 One of al-Ṣafā and al-Marwah, the two hills next to the Kaaba.

Ḥārith, for example, was someone who tried to oppose the Muslims, by piecing together fabricated reports from different books he had read.

The Prophet ﷺ did not make a habit of being absent from his people, nor did he make many journeys to the lands of the Christians or the Jews. Some have claimed that he learnt from them, but Prophet Muhammad ﷺ spent his youth as a shepherd, as was the custom of Prophets. After that, he only travelled away from the land of the Arabs on one or two occasions, and even then, he did not stay long enough to learn a small amount from them, let alone great endeavours! The Prophet ﷺ would always travel in the company of his people and his tribe, and this situation did not change for the duration of his time in Makkah. He never visited a rabbi, priest, astrologer, or fortune-teller. Even if he had done so, his arrival with the miracle of the Qur'an would have cut off every excuse, refuted every argument, and settled every affair.

Interactions of the Prophet ﷺ with the Angels and the Jinn

One of the most mesmerizing and miraculous characteristics of the Prophet ﷺ was his special ability in communicating with unseen beings; Allah supplied him with reinforcements from the ranks of the angels, and subdued the jinn into obeying him.

Allah Exalted confirms that these interactions took place in several passages in the Qur'an:

"But if you continue to collaborate against him, then know that Allah Himself is his Guardian. And Gabriel, the righteous believers, and the angels are all his supporters as well."[551] "Remember, O Prophet, when your Lord revealed to the angels, 'I am with you. So make the believers stand firm.'"[552]

---

551 *al-Taḥrīm*, 4.

552 *al-Anfāl*, 12.

"Remember when you cried out to your Lord for help, He answered, 'I will reinforce you with a thousand angels – followed by many others' And Allah made this sign a victory and reassurance to your hearts. Victory comes only from Allah. Surely Allah is Almighty, All-Wise."[553]

"Remember, O Prophet, when We sent a group of jinn your way to listen to the Qur'an. Then, upon hearing it, they said to one another, 'Listen quietly!' Then when it was over, they returned to their fellow jinn as warners."[554]

I heard the following hadith from Sufyān ibn al-ʿĀṣī, who narrated from Abū al-Layth al-Samarqandī, from ʿAbd al-Ghāfir al-Fārisī, from Abū Aḥmad al-Julūdī, from Ibn Sufyān, from Muslim, from ʿUbaydullāh ibn Muʿādh, from his father, from Shuʿbah, from Sulayman al-Shaybānī, from Zirr ibn Ḥubaysh, that ʿAbdullāh ibn Masʿūd said, concerning the statement of Allah Exalted: "He certainly saw some of his Lord's greatest signs",[555] that the Prophet ﷺ saw Jibrīl in his true form, with six hundred wings on his back.[556]

The hadiths describing the interactions of the Prophet ﷺ with Jibrīl, Isrāfīl, and other angels are well-known, including the magnificent form and number of the angels he witnessed on the Night Journey. Jibrīl was seen in more than one form; witnessed by different groups of the Companions at different times. For example, he was observed in the form of a man, asking the Prophet ﷺ for definitions of Islam and īmān.[557]

Ibn ʿAbbās, Usāmah ibn Zayd and others saw Jibrīl in the form of a man who resembled Diḥyah ibn Khalīfah al-Kalbī, an incredibly hand-

---

553 *al-Anfāl*, 9-10.

554 *al-Aḥqāf*, 29.

555 *al-Najm*, 18.

556 The chain of the author is from Muslim (174/282). Also reported by Bukhārī (3232).

557 Reported by Bukhārī (50) and Muslim (9, 10) from Abū Hurayrah, and by Muslim (8) from ʿUmar ibn al-Khaṭṭāb.

some Companion who served as an envoy to the Prophet ﷺ.[558] Sa'd reports seeing Jibrīl and Mīkā'īl as two men, to his left and his right, clothed in white garments.[559] Similar reports were recorded from other sources. Some Companions heard the angels urging them on and rebuffing their enemies at the Battle of Badr.[560] They saw the enemies' heads flying, but could not see who had attacked them.[561] During the same battle, Abū Sufyān ibn al-Ḥārith saw two men riding piebald horses – black-coated with splotches of white – somehow hovering between the earth and the sky.[562]

The angels would greet and shake hands with 'Imrān ibn al-Ḥuṣayn.[563] When the Prophet ﷺ showed Jibrīl to Ḥamzah, at the Kaaba, his uncle passed out from the shock.[564] On the night of the jinn, when a group of them gathered to hear the recitation of the Prophet ﷺ, 'Abdullāh ibn Mas'ūd saw them and heard them conversing with each other, likening their appearance to the people of Zuṭṭ[565].

Ibn Sa'd mentioned that when Muṣ'ab ibn 'Umayr was martyred at

---

558 The vision of Ibn 'Abbās was mentioned by Haythamī in *Majma' al-Zawā'id* (9/276), and he said: "It was related by Ṭabarānī, and the chain contains unknown narrators." Haythamī also mentions it without the reference to Diḥyah (9/276), and he said: "It was related by Aḥmad and Ṭabarānī from multiple chains, and the narrators are sound." See also, Tirmidhī (3822). Also reported by Bukhārī (4980) and Muslim (2451).

559 Reported by Bukhārī (4054) and Muslim (2306) from Sa'd ibn Abī Waqqāṣ.

560 Reported by Muslim (1763) from Ibn 'Abbās.

561 Related by Ṭabarānī from the hadith of Sahl ibn Ḥunayf. Haythamī said in *Majma' al-Zawā'id* (6/84): "The chain contains Muhammad ibn Yaḥyā al-Iskandarānī; Ibn Yūnus said that he narrated *munkar* hadiths." Also reported by Aḥmad (5/450) from Abū Dāwūd al-Māzinī. Haythamī said in *Majma' al-Zawā'id* (6/83): "The chain contains narrators who are not named." Also reported by Bayhaqī in *Al-Dalā'il* (see *Al-Manāhil*, p. 862).

562 Reported by al-Wāqidī in *Al-Maghāzī* (1/76) and Bayhaqī in *Al-Dalā'il*, from Suhayl ibn 'Amr, who said that he was the one who saw it.

563 Related by Ibn Sa'd from Qatādah (see *Al-Manāhil*, p. 864). Also reported by Muslim (1226/167).

564 A *mursal* hadith. Related by Bayhaqī from 'Ammār ibn Abī 'Ammār (see *Al-Manāhil*, p. 865).

565 al-Zuṭṭ: a dark-skinned tribe, originally descending from India before moving to the Persian Gulf. Related by Bayhaqī (see *Al-Manāhil*, p. 866). Also see the hadith about the gathering of the jinn, found in Muslim (450) and *Majma' al-Zawā'id* (8/313-315).

the Battle of Uḥud, an angel resembling his appearance took up the battle flag. The Prophet ﷺ called: "Mus'ab! Press forward!" but he replied, "I am not Mus'ab." The Prophet ﷺ realized he was an angel.[566]

'Umar ibn al-Khaṭṭāb said: "We were sitting with the Prophet ﷺ when an old man arrived, carrying a stick in his hand. He exchanged greetings with the Prophet ﷺ, who said: 'You have the voice of a jinn. Who are you?' The man gave his name as Hāmah ibn al-Hīm ibn Lāqis ibn Iblīs. In a lengthy hadith, he mentioned that he had previously met with the Prophet Nūḥ, and other Prophets after him.[567] The Messenger of Allah ﷺ taught him some surahs from the Qur'an.

Al-Wāqidī relates that when Khālid ibn al-Walīd destroyed the statue of al-'Uzzā, a false deity belonging to the idol-worshippers, a naked woman came running towards him with her hair flying, and he cut her down with his sword. He informed the Prophet ﷺ of what had happened, and he told Khālid: "That was al-'Uzzā."[568]

The Messenger of Allah ﷺ said: "Yesterday, Shayṭān came to interrupt my prayer, but Allah empowered me to overcome. I grabbed him, and I wanted to tie him to one of the posts of the mosque so that you could all see him, but then I remembered the supplication of my brother, the Prophet Sulaymān: '"My Lord! Forgive me, and grant me an authority that will never be matched by anyone after me. You indeed are the Giver of all bounties."'[569] Instead, the Shayṭān was sent packing, utterly humiliated."[570]

Again, this is an expansive topic.

---

566 The author attributed it to Ibn Sa'd. Also reported by Ibn Abī Shaybah in *Al-Muṣannaf*, with a weak chain (see *Al-Manāhil*, p. 867).

567 Related by Bayhaqī, al-'Uqaylī, and others.

568 Also reported by Nasā'ī in *Al-Kubrā*, Bayhaqī in *Al-Dalā'il*, Ṭabarānī, and Abū Ya'lā (902), from the hadith of Abū al-Ṭufayl. Haythamī said in *Majma' al-Zawā'id* (6/176): "It was related by Ṭabarānī; the chain contains Yaḥyā ibn al-Mundhir, who is a weak narrator."

569 *Ṣād*, 35.

570 Reported by Bukhārī (461) and Muslim (541) from Abū Hurayrah.

Descriptions from Jewish and Christian Scholars and Ascetics of the Prophet ﷺ and his Community

Furthermore, the reports that have reached us from the monks, ascetics, and scholars of the People of the Book – describing and predicting the name of the Prophet ﷺ, the marks he would bear, his characteristics, and those of his community – confirm his Prophethood and Messengership. They mentioned the seal of the Prophets that would be found between his shoulder blades. Other information was recorded in the poetry of those who believed in One Creator before the Prophet ﷺ was sent with revelation: the poetry of Tubbaʿ[571], al-Aws ibn Ḥārithah[572], Kaʿb ibn Lu'ayy[573], Sufyān ibn Mujāshiʿ, Quss ibn Sāʿidah[574], Sayf ibn Dhī Yazan[575], and others.

Others who foretold aspects of the Prophethood of our Master Muhammad ﷺ include Zayd ibn ʿAmr ibn Nufayl[576], Waraqah ibn Nawfal[577], ʿAthkalān al-Ḥimyarī, and many Jewish scholars. Some of what they predicted was taken from the Torah and the Gospel, and elaborated on by wise people from their community. Those from amongst them

571 The nickname of a great leader and King of the Himyarites, in Yemen.

572 He was al-Aws ibn Ḥārithah ibn Thaʿlabah, the grandfather of the Aws tribe. His biography can be found in *Al-Aʿlām*.

573 An ancestor of the Prophet ﷺ; he died in 173 BH. His biography can be found in *Al-Aʿlām*.

574 A famous orator; he died in 23 BH. His biography can be found in *Al-Iṣābah*.

575 A Himayrite King from Yemen; he died in 50 BH. His biography can be found in *Al-Aʿlām*.

576 The father of the noble Companion, Saʿīd ibn Zayd. He did not live to see Islam. He used to worship Allah Exalted according to the religion of Prophet Ibrāhīm. He met the Prophet ﷺ but died five years before he received revelation. The Prophet ﷺ was asked about him afterwards, and he said: "We will be raised from the same nation on the Day of Judgement." See also, *Al-Aʿlām*.

577 He was the paternal cousin of Khadījah, Mother of the Believers. He died in 12 BH, and his biography can be found in *Al-Iṣābah* and *Al-Aʿlām*. The story of his prediction about the Prophet ﷺ was mentioned by Ṭabarī, Baghawī, Ibn Qāniʿ, Ibn al-Sakan, Ibn Ḥajr, and others.

who became Muslim include ʿAbdullāh ibn Salām[578], the three sons of Saʿyah[579], Yāmīn ibn Yāmīn[580], Mukhayrīq[581], Kaʿb al-Aḥbār, and others like them. There were also Christian scholars who embraced Islam, including Bahīrā[582], Nasṭūr al-Ḥabashah, the friend of Buṣrā, Ḍaghāṭir[583], the Bishops of Syria, al-Jārūd[584], Salmān[585], Tamīm[586], the Negus[587] and the Christians of Ethiopia, the Bishops of Najrān, and others.

Despite their refusal to accept Islam, many of their leaders also attested to the truthfulness of the Prophet ﷺ, including Heraclius, the Pope and Muqawqis[588], Ibn Ṣūriyā, Ibn Akhṭab and his brother, Kaʿb ibn Asad[589], al-Zabīr ibn Bāṭiyā al-Quraẓī[590], and other Jewish scholars whose sense of envy and antagonism prevented them from following the right path.

---

578 He was a Jewish rabbi before entering Islam, and he died in Madinah in 43 AH.

579 They were Zayd, Thaʿlabah and Usayd ibn Saʿyah, or "Saʿnah". They were Jews who became Muslim.

580 He was from the People of the Book who embraced Islam. There was some difference of opinion about his father's name, and his biography can be found in *Usd al-Ghābah*.

581 A well-known and wealthy Jewish rabbi who became Muslim, and was martyred at the Battle of Uḥud. His story can be found in the *Sīrah* of Ibn Hishām (1/518).

582 The story is reported by Tirmidhī (3620) and Ḥākim (2/615-616) from Abū Mūsā al-Ashʿarī. Tirmidhī said: "This hadith is *ḥasan gharīb*." Ḥākim authenticated the hadith, but Dhahabī did not concur.

583 He was a Roman bishop, and he became Muslim when he read the letter that the Prophet ﷺ had sent to Caesar.

584 His name is Bishr ibn ʿAmr al-ʿAbdī. He was a Christian who embraced Islam, and he died as a martyr, in Persia, in 20 AH. See *Al-Aʿlām*.

585 Salmān al-Fārisī, the noble Companion. He was originally from Aṣbahān, and he died in 34 AH.

586 Tamīm al-Dārī, the noble Companion. A dedicated worshipper from the people of Palestine, it is said that he died in 40 AH.

587 Al-Najāshī, the nickname of all the Kings of Ethiopia. The Najāshī intended here was Aṣḥamah, who accepted Islam. The Prophet ﷺ prayed his funeral prayer in his absence.

588 The leaders of the Catholic and Coptic communities respectively.

589 Kaʿb ibn Asad ibn Saʿīd al-Quraẓī, from the tribe of Banū Qurayẓah. His story can be found in the *Sīrah* of Ibn Hishām (2/235).

590 He was one of the most learned men from the Jews. He was killed at the Siege of the Banū Qurayẓah as a disbeliever. His story can be found in the *Sīrah* of Ibn Hishām (2/244-245).

It hurt the Christians and Jews to admit that the Prophet ﷺ and his followers were accurately described in their books. The Prophet ﷺ used what was contained in their scriptures as an evidence against them, and rebuked them for altering, concealing and twisting the words contained therein. The Prophet ﷺ invited these opponents of Islam to supplicate alongside him, for Allah to curse whichever party was hiding the truth. No-one dared to formally confront the Prophet ﷺ, for fear of having to shine a light on what their books really contained. If they had been able to prove that their scriptures contradicted what the Prophet ﷺ was claiming, it would have been easier for them, but instead they had their houses destroyed, lost their wealth and their lives, and, ultimately, gave up the fight anyway. They had been instructed to bring scriptural evidence to support their accusations against the Prophet ﷺ: "Say, 'Bring the Torah and read it, if your claims are true.'"[591]

We also have the warnings of fortune-tellers such as Shāfiʿ ibn Kulayb, Shiqq[592], Saṭīḥ[593], Sawād ibn Qārib[594], Khunāfir[595], al-Afʿā al-Jurhumī[596], Jidhl ibn Jidhl al-Kindī, Ibn Khalaṣah al-Dawsī, Suʿdā bint Kurayz[597], Fāṭimah bint al-Nuʿmān, as well as many we have not mentioned.

Not to mention what was heard from the false idols about his Prophethood, and the time of his Messengership; in fact, it was the voices of jinn that were heard. The name of the Prophet ﷺ and attestations to his status

---

591 Āl ʿImrān, 93.

592 He was Shiqq ibn Ṣaʿb al-Azdī, an ignorant fortune-teller. He died in 55 BH. See also, *Al-Aʿlām*.

593 He was Rabīʿah ibn Rabīʿah, an ignorant fortune-teller from the Ghassanids. He died in 52 BH. See also, *Al-Aʿlām*.

594 He was a fortune-teller and a poet in the days of ignorance, and then a Companion in Islam. He died in 15 AH. See also, *Al-Aʿlām*.

595 A fortune-teller from Ḥimyar. He became a Muslim at the hand of Muʿādh ibn Jabal, .

596 A sage from the ancient Jurhum tribe. See also, *Al-Aʿlām*.

597 The maternal aunt of ʿUthmān ibn ʿAffān. She was a fortune-teller in the days of ignorance, and then a Companion in Islam. Her biography can be found in *Al-Iṣābah*, and *A*ʿlām al-*Nisā'*.

were found in ancient etchings and engravings. Many people have become Muslim after seeing these signs.

Signs that Appeared at the Birth of the Prophet ﷺ

There were miraculous signs at the birth of the Prophet ﷺ, and they were related by his mother and others who were present. Ḥalīmah al-Sa'diyyah, the wet-nurse of the Prophet ﷺ, mentions him lifting his head when he had just been born, and raising his eyes to the heavens. al-'Irbāḍ ibn Sāriyah described a light emanating as he was born. Umm 'Uthmān ibn Abī al-Āṣ added that the light was so piercing it obscured her sight, and that there were shooting stars in the sky.[598] The midwife, Umm 'Abd al-Raḥmān ibn 'Awf, said: "When the Prophet ﷺ first fell into my hands as a baby, he sneezed, and I heard a voice say: 'May Allah have mercy on you.' Everything between the east and the west was illuminated before my eyes, until I could see as far as the castles of the Romans."[599]

Ḥalīmah and her husband both recognized the blessings that arrived with the Prophet ﷺ when they took him into their care; the abundance of her milk, the milk of their elderly female camel, the fertility of their sheep, and the vitality and excellent character of our Master Muhammad ﷺ as he grew up.

There were miracles that occurred on the night of his birth: the throne arch of Khosrow shuddered, and the fourteen balconies of his palace suddenly collapsed; the waters of Lake Tiberias receded; the flame of the Zoroastrians, which had not been extinguished for one thousand years, went

598 Related by Ṭabarānī. Haythamī says in *Majma' al-Zawā'id* (8/220): "The chain contains 'Abd al-'Azīz ibn 'Imrān, and he was left because of his unreliabilty (*matrūk*)." See *Al-Manāhil*, p. 874.

599 Related by Abū Nu'aym in *Al-Dalā'il* from 'Abd al-Raḥmān ibn 'Awf, from his mother (the midwife).

out;[600] and the heavens were guarded with shooting stars, cutting off the jinn from listening in.

It was reported that when the Prophet ﷺ, as a child, ate with his uncle Abū Ṭālib and his family, they would all feel quenched and satiated, but when he was not present, they would continue to eat without feeling full. Most of the children of Abū Ṭālib would awaken in the morning in a disheveled state, but the Prophet ﷺ would appear with glowing skin and bright eyes.[601] Umm Ayman, the maid of the Prophet ﷺ, said: "I never saw him complain of hunger or thirst, neither as a child or as an adult."[602]

Even at a young age, the Prophet ﷺ was imbued with an aversion to the false idols worshipped by the Quraysh, and the misguided customs of the pre-Islamic period. Allah instilled these special qualities in His Messenger ﷺ and protected him even in regard to his modesty. As the story goes, when the Kaaba was rebuilt, the Prophet ﷺ removed his *izār*[603], leaving himself exposed, so that he could place it on his shoulders as he lifted stones. Suddenly, he fell to the ground, and his *izār* dropped back into place, covering the lower half of his body again. His uncle asked what had happened, and the Prophet ﷺ replied: "I have been protected from nudity."[604]

When the Prophet ﷺ travelled, the clouds would protect him from the heat. Khadījah and her companions once witnessed the Prophet ﷺ approaching, with two angels shading him. When she told Maysarah, she

---

600 Related by Bayhaqī, Ibn Abī al-Dunyā, and Ibn al-Sakan, in *Maʿrifat al-Ṣaḥābah*, from Makhzūm ibn Hānī' al-Makhzūmī. See *Al-Manāhil*, p. 876.

601 Related by Ibn Saʿd from Ibn ʿAbbās, and Mujāhid and Ismāʿīl from Abū Ḥabībah, in a lengthy hadith. See *Al-Manāhil*, p. 877.

602 Related by Ibn Saʿd and Abū Nuʿaym in *Al-Dalā'il* (see also, *Al-Manāhil*, 878). Umm Ayman was Barakah al-Ḥabashiyyah, the wife of Zayd ibn Ḥārithah.

603 A garment wrapped around the lower half of the body, similar to a sarong.

604 Similar was reported by Bukhārī (364) and Muslim (360) from Jābir ibn ʿAbdullāh, and Suyūṭī extends the chain to Bayhaqī, from Ibn ʿAbbās, in *Al-Manāhil*, p. 879.

confirmed that she had seen the same thing happening on their journeys together.[605] Ḥalīmah narrated a similar case when the Prophet ﷺ was in her care[606] and one of her sons said the same.

On one of his journeys, before he had received divine revelation, the Prophet ﷺ stopped off under a dried-out tree. Moments later, the surroundings sprung to life, vegetation sprouted from the ground and blossomed,[607] and the branches of the tree drooped over him. Some narrations mention that the shade of the tree inclined towards him.

It was said that the Prophet ﷺ did not cast a shadow under the Sun or the Moon.[608] Flies would never land on his body or his clothes.[609] He had a propensity for seeking solitude, until he started receiving revelation.[610] During his final illness, he warned the people that his death was approaching,[611] and that his body was to be buried at his home[612] in Madinah.[613] He said that between his home and the minbar, in the mosque of Madinah, was a garden from the gardens of Paradise.[614]

Allah gave him a choice concerning his death.[615] The angels prayed over his body, and the Angel of Death asked for permission, which he had never

---

605 Related by Ibn Sa'd from Nafīsah bint Munyah.

606 Related by al-Wāqidī, Ibn Sa'd, and Ibn 'Asākir, from Ibn 'Abbās.

607 Mentioned by Suyūṭī in *Al-Manāhil*, p. 883 without mentioning the narrator. Al-Dalajiyy said: "I do not know who related it."

608 Reported by Ḥakīm al-Tirmidhī in *Nawādir al-Uṣūl*. The chain contains 'Abd al-Raḥmān ibn Qays, and he was a liar, and 'Abd al-Malik ibn 'Abdullāh, and he was unknown.

609 Mentioned by Suyūṭī in *Al-Manāhil*, p. 886 without mentioning the narrator, and in *Nasīm al-Riyāḍ*.

610 Taken from the hadith about the first onset of revelation, reported by Bukhārī (3) and Muslim (160) from 'Ā'ishah.

611 Reported by Bukhārī (6186) and Muslim (2450) from the hadith of 'Ā'ishah from Fāṭimah.

612 Related by Bayhaqī in *Al-Dalā'il* from the hadith of Abū Bakr.

613 Related by Abū Nu'aym in *Al-Dalā'il* from Ma'qil ibn Yasār.

614 See *Jāmi' al-Uṣūl* (9/329).

615 Reported by Bukhārī (6348) and Muslim (2444) from the hadith of 'Ā'ishah, and Bukhārī (466) from al-Khudrī.

done before.[616] The people preparing his body for the grave heard a voice calling them not to remove his garment when they washed him.[617] When the Prophet ﷺ passed away, al-Khiḍr[618] and the angels consoled his family.

The Companions recognized his blessings both during his life, and after his death. ʿUmar would ask the uncle of the Prophet ﷺ, al-ʿAbbās, to supplicate for rain when they were threatened with drought,[619] and many sought the blessings of his descendants.

The Superiority of the Miracles of the Final Prophet ﷺ

To conclude, in this chapter we have presented a plethora of clear miracles that the Prophet ﷺ performed, and detailed many compelling signs of his Prophethood. Had we mentioned just one of these signs, it would have sufficed as evidence. In order to achieve our purpose, we have condensed longer hadiths, and omitted many others. We have shortened chains of transmission where appropriate, and confined ourselves to the narrations of the most prominent scholars. Had this not been the case, the topic at hand would have filled several volumes.

The miracles of the Final Prophet ﷺ were more manifest than those of Messengers preceding him from two perspectives. Firstly, they were far greater in number. For every miracle that any Prophet before him had performed, the Final Prophet ﷺ came with a miracle that was either similar, or more powerful. Many people have mentioned this to be the case, but if the reader wants to confirm, they should revise the sections of this

---

616 Related by al-Shāfiʿī in his *Sunan*, al-ʿAdanī in his *Musnad*, Bayhaqī in *Al-Dalā'il*. ʿIrāqī said in *Takhrīj Aḥādīth al-Iḥyā'* (4/473): "It is *munkar*." See also, *Majma' al-Zawā'id* (9/ 25-36).

617 Reported by Abū Dāwūd (3140) and others, from the hadith of ʿĀ'ishah. Authenticated by Ibn Ḥibbān in *Mawārid* (2156), Ḥākim, and Bayhaqī.

618 ʿIrāqī said in *Takhrīj Aḥādīth al-Iḥyā'* (4/474): "As for whoever mentioned al-Khiḍr in the condolences, know that Nawawī denied his presence in the books of hadith. It was related by Ḥākim in *Al-Mustadrak*, but he did not authenticate it."

619 Reported by Bukhārī (1010) from Anas ibn Mālik.

very chapter, and compare what they contain to the miracles of previous Prophets. That is one way to come to the truth, if Allah wills.

As for the statement that his miracles were many, then look at the example of the Qur'an! It is a miracle in its entirety. The scholars differed as to the smallest unit of Qur'an that could be considered miraculous: some suggested the shortest surah – "We have given you, O Prophet, abundant goodness"[620] – or a verse of a similar length. Others said that any verse could be considered so, regardless of its length. A third group went one step further, arguing that every sentence enunciated in the Qur'an was miraculous, even if it consisted of only one or two words.

The truth, and the minimum challenge set down to the enemies of Islam, is contained in the command of Allah: "Tell them O Prophet, 'Produce one surah like it then'".[621] Let us consider that the Qur'an contains approximately seventy-seven thousand words – although there is some difference of opinion[622] – and Surah al-Kawthar contains ten. By that calculation, the Qur'an can be divided into more than seven thousand units, each the size of one surah, and each one absolutely inimitable. As we mentioned before, the Qur'an is a miraculous book from two perspectives; its eloquence and its composition. In this way, every unit contains two miracles. The number we cited above can, therefore, be doubled. On top of that, each surah may contain reports pertaining to the Unseen, with each report comprising a miracle in itself, so the number can be multiplied again. Eventually, you come to realize that it is impossible to place a limit on the vast store of evidence the Qur'an encompasses.

---

620 *al-Kawthar*, 1.

621 *Yūnus*, 38.

622 Al-Zurqānī said, in *Manāhil al-'Irfān* (1/348): "Some mentioned that the Qur'an contains 77,934 words, and others differed. The difference of opinion stems from words differing in their surface and metaphorical meanings, and differing in their spoken and written forms. Therefore, the opinions are all valid."

Secondly, the miracles of the Prophet ﷺ were clear-cut. Messengers before him were consistently given the ability to perform miracles consonant with the people of the time, and the advances in civilization most pertinent to that generation. At the time of the Prophet Mūsā, magic was the most prominent topic amongst the people. So, he was sent with miracles that resembled what his enemies claimed to be able to do with magic. When they, inevitably, could not replicate the miracles of Mūsā, their claims to power were undermined, and their magic was debased. At the time of the Prophet ʿĪsā, the most significant developments were in the field of medicine. So, he came with medical miracles they never would have thought possible; bringing dead people back to life, gifting sight to those born blind, and curing leprosy without any medicine or treatment. And other Prophets followed the same blueprint, being gifted the category of miracles that would impact their people the most.

Finally, Allah sent the Prophet Muhammad ﷺ. The Arabs were advanced in four areas: rhetoric, poetry, storytelling, and fortune-telling. The Qur'an was revealed to the Prophet ﷺ, completely outstripping their specialisms with its purity of language; concision; eloquence; and literary style, which did not match with anything that had come before. The Qur'an had a wondrous, unique style which the Arabs could not recognize from amongst the meters of poetry and genres of prose they were familiar with. This book contained information about different beings, events, concealed secrets, and hidden thoughts. Everything it said was proven true, and even the most stubborn opponents had no choice but to confirm its reliability as a source of information. Therefore, the fortune-tellers were destroyed, because whereas the Qur'an was consistently accurate, they were lucky to get something correct once for every ten attempts. One source of the fortune-tellers' information was the jinn who would snatch bites of information by sneakily listening in to the heavens; this source was cut off and uprooted by the shooting stars and meteors which targeted the jinn. The Qur'an combined news of previous generations and Prophets, past events, and nations that were destroyed, in a way that even those who devoted themselves to historical study could not. This is a miraculous book that will continue to guide until the Day of Judgement, and a proof for future generations. The truth cannot be hidden from the one who contemplates its meanings.

In the context of any period, if you were to study the predictions found in the Qur'an, you would have no choice but to testify to its truthfulness. Faith is renewed and increased, and its proofs are made clear to all. As the saying goes, the one who hears is not like the one who sees, and to witness with your own eyes increases you in certainty. The soul is raised in tranquility, from possessing the knowledge of certainty, to the vision of certainty.

Most miracles came to an end with the death of their Messenger. In contrast, the miracle of our Prophet ﷺ will never cease or die out, and his signs are consistently renewed, and will never wither away. According to the strongest opinion, and most apparent meaning, this is what the Prophet ﷺ was alluding to in a hadith narrated to us by the esteemed Abū ʿAlī, from Abū al-Walīd, from Abū Dharr, from Abū Muhammad, Abū Isḥāq, and Abū al-Haytham. They said: "It was narrated to us from from al-Farabrī, from Bukhārī, from ʿAbd al-ʿAzīz ibn ʿAbdullāh, from al-Layth, from Saʿīd, from his father, from Abū Hurayrah , that the Prophet ﷺ said: 'Every Prophet was given signs that his people believed in. Allah inspired me with a revelation, and I hope to be the Prophet with the most followers on the Day of Judgement.'"[623]

That is the interpretation of many scholars, and it is the most evident and authentic opinion, if Allah wills. Other scholars adopted an alternative interpretation of this hadith. Rather than referring to only the revelation

623 The chain of the author is from Bukhārī (7274).

and speech the Prophet ﷺ was sent with, there is a deeper meaning. When other Messengers were sent with miracles, their most obstinate and dogged opponents attempted to sow doubt into weak minds by attempting to imitate those miracles. For example, at the time of Prophet Mūsā, the magicians' "ropes and staffs appeared to him – by their magic – to be slithering."[624] The magicians also had other methods and objects they used to deceive people. The Qur'an, in contrast, is completely free of trickery, magic or deception. From this perspective, it was the clearest miracle people had witnessed. In any case, whilst the latter interpretation presents some points of objection, the first view seems closest to the truth. The two opinions accepted by the people of the Sunnah both agree that although bringing something like the Qur'an is within the scope of a human being's capabilities, it has never been achieved, and will never be achieved in the future. That is because Allah Exalted has not allowed human beings to do so.

There is a clear distinction between the two schools of thought. Regardless of which opinion is accepted, the Arabs gave up on their attempts to imitate the Qur'an. Instead, they settled for hardship, exile, capture, and humiliation. They experienced devastating changes in their circumstances, as well as the loss of lives and wealth, and were completely incapable of mounting any response, as they found themselves on the receiving end of condemnation and reprimand. To put themselves through such trials, rather than replicate a single surah of the Qur'an, is the clearest sign that they could not do so. It may have been within their capabilities, but Allah had prevented them.

This is the view that was adopted by the great scholar Abū al-Maʿālī al-Juwaynī, and others. He said: We consider this to be a more comprehensive way of outstripping the norms of society than through captivating actions alone, as with the transformation of the staff into a snake, and the

---

624 Ṭāhā, 66.

likes of it. These actions can fool the viewer into believing the miracle was only possible because the one performing it had an expertise in the field; in this example, an expertise in magic. That is until they research the matter further, and realize the error in their judgement. As for the challenge of the Qur'an, presented to human beings over centuries, to bring something from the same category of speech that they produce but that resembles the revelation, they were unable to do so. The only explanation for this, is that Allah prevented His creation from imitating the Qur'an. Imagine if a Prophet had said, "my sign is that Allah will prevent people from standing up, even though they are free of disease and have the ability to do so", and then it happened just as he had predicted. Surely, that would be a mesmerizing sign and an indisputable proof. Success is with Allah.

There were some scholars who failed to appreciate the superiority of the miracles of the Final Prophet ﷺ above the miracles of Prophets before him. Instead, they came up with the excuse that the Prophet ﷺ had come to the Arabs with the miracle of the Qur'an because of their deep understanding, sharp intellect, and linguistic perspicacity. According to this view, the Arabs used their knowledge and expertise to comprehend the miraculous nature of the Qur'an. Other nations such as the Copts, the Banū Isrā'īl, and others, did not have the same intellectual capacity. These communities were prone to falling into misguidance; the Pharoah managed to convince them that he was their Lord; al-Sāmirī persuaded them to abandon their faith and worship a statue of a golden calf instead; and they began to worship the Messiah[625] after coming to a consensus that he had been crucified, when "But they neither killed him nor crucified him – it was only made to appear so."[626] Because of their ignorance and obstinate nature, Mūsā came to them with clear, manifest signs that left absolutely

---

625 'Īsā ibn Maryam.

626 *al-Nisā'*, 157.

no room for doubt. Yet, they still managed to say, "'We will never believe you until we see Allah with our own eyes.'"[627] They were not satisfied with the manna and quails that had been sent to them, and instead substituted worse for better.[628]

The Arabs, despite their ignorance, were more likely to recognize their Maker, and they sought the intercession of their false idols as a means of getting closer to Allah. Some of them believed in worshipping Allah without partners even before the Messenger ﷺ came, having arrived at their conclusions through intellectual argument and spiritual reflection. Because of this, when the Messenger ﷺ conveyed the Book of Allah to them, they understood its wisdom and miraculous nature. They believed in the message of the Qur'an, and with every passing day their faith increased. They were willing to abandon the material world completely; to migrate and leave their homes and possessions behind; and to fight alongside the Prophet ﷺ, even if it was against their own parents and children.

There are many paths to expound further on this topic, but we will suffice with the elucidation of the miracles of our Prophet ﷺ that has preceded.

With Allah, I seek help. He is enough for me, and an Excellent Protector.

---

627 *al-Baqarah*, 55.

628 A reference to *al-Baqarah*, 61.

Made in the USA
Coppell, TX
04 February 2026

71037635R00094